Her Shattered Heart

By Mary DeWeber

Published by Avery Anne Publishers
www.averyannepublishers.org

ISBN-13: 978-0692324417
ISBN-10: 0692324410

Chapter 1

"Miss Hanson will you come in here please?"

Cassie smiled at the irritation that seeped through the intercom with her employer's voice. What had he misplaced this time she wondered as she entered his office?

Logan Blake raised startling blue eyes ripe with impatience to Cassie's calm face.

"Where have you hidden the Johnson file?" he scowled.

"Where I always hide things from you." Crossing to the bank of filing cabinets she retrieved the requested file and handed it to him.

"I don't see why you have to file everything before I'm finished with it." The tension in his voice was already beginning to fade.

"You know I only file the things you put in here." She tapped the basket clearly marked 'file'. "Every thing else gets stacked neatly waiting your return, the same as always."

"Sorry, I know I'm like a bear with a sore head this morning, I'm afraid I was up late working on today's proposal." A boyish smile softened the angular planes of his face and accentuated the deep dimples in his lean cheeks. His eyes were the kind you could cheerfully get lost in, deep blue with thick dark lashes under straight brows. In his irritation he had ruffled his slightly wavy dark hair and as always when that happened her fingers itched to smooth it back into place. Yawning widely he stretched well-

1

muscled arms over his head and getting to his feet towered over her.

"What would I do without you?" He asked as he placed the folder that she had handed him in his brief case.

"You mean besides lose everything, be late to every meeting and generally watch your business fall apart?" She joked.

"Touché, I give up." He grinned raising his hands in mock defeat. "I don't want to argue today, but I have a feeling the board isn't going to like what I'm about to propose."

"They usually don't," she said dryly

Eyeing her critically he asked. "Are you ready?"

"Yes Mr. Blake." Slipping into a more formal attitude she went to her office and gathered the things needed for his presentation then followed him to the boardroom.

Cassie had worked for Blake International for the past five years, the last two of which she had spent as his assistant. Working with Logan Blake had taught her a deep respect for the grueling aspects of owning an international company. At thirty-three Logan had taken the business his father started and turned it into a multi-million dollar venture. He had an uncanny knack for knowing which of the thousands of inventions sent to the company each year were worth investing in. Quite often he'd had to fight the board members over the money spent to research and test each item before releasing it to the public. Today was no exception.

"Mr. Blake, I respect your desire for safety, but sometimes I think you're more interested in the technical aspects of these inventions than is necessary. This is one of those times." Charlie Parker, Logan Internationals financial advisor chose his words carefully. "The projected cost of this project is almost double what it should be and I advise cutting back on research."

"Need I remind you that safety is of utmost importance?" Logan asked. "I personally don't want to be responsible for possible injuries and we don't need a rash of lawsuits. I've reviewed the proposed cuts and I have some revisions myself to share with you. Miss Hanson?" Cassie passed the proposals around and they got down to the business at hand.

Cassie admired her employers keen business sense. Of the many times she had sat in this boardroom watching him in action, she'd never tired of it. Rather she had learned about the business and had been able to anticipate what Logan would need the next time he went into battle.

Consequently, they worked well together. Cassie already knew what the outcome of today's foray would be long before the meeting drew to an end. Logan would once again be the victor in the corporate games.

Back in the office his jubilation was obvious. "We did it Cass. We saved the project." He smiled widely as he sat on the corner of her desk. "Why don't you let your hair down and take the afternoon off with me? We could picnic in the park," he grinned widely. "Boy, I could use the fresh air."

"Sorry, but I can't do that." She discouraged him.

"Can't what, come out to lunch or let your hair down?" His appraising look took in her thick curly auburn hair tightly secured in its customary French twist. He'd always had an insane desire to remove her hairpins and let it fall free. Her slight features were intriguing. The thick-fringed expressive green eyes over a piquant nose suggested merriment, while her mobile mouth could either hold a professional smile or quirk into a grin at a moment's notice. He had come to look forward to those brief glimpses into the lighter side of her character. How he longed to see beneath the cool facade she presented. Her severe suits were always long sleeved with either a skirt well below the knees or with slacks that hid her willowy figure. Even when he teased a smile or good-natured banter out of her, he had never been able to get past her basic reserve.

"Both," she brought him back to reality and put a damper on his thoughts. "I have too much to do this afternoon to take time off for a picnic, and I never let my hair down."

"I was thinking…" He used the phrase that often precluded his moments of lighthearted banter.

"That's a frightening proposition." Cassie coolly observed as she slipped into her role as straight man.

"You're interrupting."

"Can you blame me? These forays into your thought process are usually long winded."

"Oh, come now," he teased. " There's generally always a point to my 'forays'."

"Stick to one thought at a time. Now, you were thinking," she admonished.

"I was thinking that it would do you good to get some sun, you're too pale." Amused at her outraged glance he pushed. "You could use a few freckles to go with that red hair." His grin widened at her expression. "I'll bet you are trying to cover up a whole bevy of freckles." Pulling out a snowy handkerchief he made as if to wipe the end of her nose.

"My hair isn't red and I don't think freckles would be professional," she said stiffly as she dodged his hand. "Now if you would excuse me, I have work to do."

"I suppose I could order you to take the rest of the day off and get some sun." He speculated as she pinned him with an icy stare. "Brr, on second thought, it's far to chilly to go outside." Turning up the collar of his jacket, he rubbed his hands together and pretended to shiver.

"Okay, back to the salt mines." He stepped away from her desk and asked, "Would you mind ordering some lunch, and get enough for both of us, I've seen what you eat and it's hardly enough to keep a bird alive." Then he disappeared into his office.

Ordering their lunch, Cassie congratulated herself on side stepping the outing. She would love to spend an afternoon with Logan, but he wouldn't understand her reluctance to expose herself to the merciless sunlight. Some things just didn't bear scrutiny.

After hanging up the telephone she indulged in an action she seldom allowed herself. With her elbows resting on her desk, she carefully she ran her fingertips over her face fingering the slight ridge that ran from within the hairline on the upper left side of her forehead diagonally down to the bridge of her nose. Pushing the painful memories away, she continued tracing the scar across her cheek to its end at the base of her jaw. Freckles weren't the only things her make-up hid. Sighing, she picked up the document before her and tried to focus on it, but it was impossible.

This was the first time Logan had commented on her make-up and it made her wonder if she was doing the right thing in hiding her scars. She had hidden behind her mask of heavy make-up for so long that she wasn't sure she wanted to let it slip. It covered more than physical scars. It was her first defense against prying eyes, a wall she had set up to keep people from getting close enough to see the woman she was no longer sure even existed. Her mask of professionalism was needed to keep her job. And without this job she couldn't possibly afford the extensive treatments she would need to reduce the ugly scars that crisscrossed her body. Dr. Jackson had been right when he'd told her that many would fade until they were hardly noticeable any longer. If only the others would fade, the inner scars that had festered for so long might heal too.

Lunch over, Cassie and Logan got down to business and plowed through the mountain of paperwork they needed to finish before the end of the day.

Once the final memo had been sent and the last of the post had gone to the mail room, Cassie breathed a sigh of relief. Looking over the open files strewn around Logan's office she began gathering the debris. Logan watched her as he spoke into the phone and when she approached his desk to place the files in their customary pile he idly placed his hand on her left wrist.

Cassie froze, she tried not to notice the way her sleeve was creeping up her arm as he absently fingered the fabric. Schooling her features into a bland mask and forcing herself to relax her arm, she tried to conquer her nervousness.

Not only was she afraid he would see the angry scars that still covered her forearm, but his warm almost caressing fingers were playing havoc with her nerves. She could feel the warmth stealing up from her toes and bringing a soft rosy glow to her neck and face.

Faking a cough she pulled away and walked across the room. Keeping her back to him she sorted through her notes. Casting a glance around the room, she walked purposefully into her office.

Cassie's knees felt weak and she slipped into her chair as she drew a shaky breath and willed her heart to calm.

This is crazy she thought. How could she have let down her guard enough to allow herself to be shaken by Logan's touch? For quite some time she had carefully avoided casual contact. He couldn't possibly feel anything more for her then a friendly employer/employee relationship. She'd better get a grip on herself right away. The last assistant who had fallen in love with Logan had found herself transferred so fast it had made her head spin. Well, she certainly had no intention of falling in love with him or anyone else for that matter.

Cassie had started working for Logan Industries fresh out of college and she had not worked her way up to her present status as personal assistant to the head of the company by being indiscreet. It had taken hard work and long hours to achieve the goals she had reached so far.

She loved keeping abreast of new developments and tracking the progress of Logan's 'pet' projects. If she kept to her present budget in six months when Logan left for his yearly visit to the London office, she would be in the position financially to resume her treatments and nothing or nobody would be allowed to stop her.

That evening she smiled to herself as she entered her apartment. Ah, home sweet home. Glancing through the mail she stepped into the small kitchen where she poured herself a glass of iced tea.

Leaving the odd collection of bills and advertisements on her kitchen table, she wandered into the living room and sinking into the couch eased off her shoes. Turning sideways so she could rest her legs on the cushions, she rubbed her tired feet together.

Even as she tried to relax and clear her mind of work she felt a now familiar unrest stealing over her. Slowly she ran her eyes over her small apartment. Small was an understatement, miniscule was closer to the truth.

The living room was barely big enough for the comfortable couch and chair she had crowded in with her TV and end table. A single window let in a little light, illuminating the mirror she used to give the room an illusion of space. There were a few pictures decorating the walls, landscapes mostly. How she longed for a larger place with room to decorate or even a window with a view, but her self imposed budget wouldn't allow for it.

There would come a day, she was sure, when there would be an end to the treatments and surgeries that had been so much a part of the last ten years of her life.

Restlessly, she sipped her iced tea and thought about the incident earlier that day. She knew she'd been uptight around Logan lately. Whenever he was near her she could feel the chemistry between them. The camaraderie they'd assumed when there was no one near was bittersweet. She felt drawn to him, as she had never been to any man before. She fought to keep all but the most mundane thoughts of him from entering her mind. To watch his rich blue eyes undergo the change from the warmth he had shown her lately, to revulsion and rejection was more than she could bear, so she had avoided making eye contact with him.

Rising, she walked the few steps to her bedroom. Standing before the full-length mirror she forced herself, as she had every day for nearly ten years, to take a dispassionate look at herself as she changed. Maybe she should try tanning again. Her five foot six inch frame wouldn't be bad if it weren't for the scars that marred her creamy skin. Dr Jackson, her plastic surgeon, had tried to get her to get into the sun for a long time now, but she hadn't wanted to expose herself to the scrutiny of anyone else. The two-inch scar on her left breast just visible above her lacy underclothes was finally fading to a faint pink line that was not nearly as wide as it had been before her last surgery. The long scar on her right thigh was still quite red as it had been deeper and required a much more extensive restoration.

Raising her arms to remove the hairpins she loosened her hair and let it fall in an auburn cloud down to her waist. Rubbing her left wrist gingerly, she felt the still tender scar that slashed about three inches above her hand. Dr. Jackson had assured her that even though, there had been some nerve damage, the soreness would eventually go away and as long as she exercised her hand and fingers there would be no lasting stiffness.

Carefully she flexed the muscles of her shoulders easing the tension. There was an itch between her shoulder blades that had bothered her on and off all day so grasping a towel at each end behind her back she carefully rubbed it slowly over the numerous scars covering her back, hips and the back of her thighs. The color and severity of the scars matched the back of her left arm.

She sighed as she reached for her favorite mint green yoga pants and matching long sleeved top. There were too many bitter memories of how people reacted upon seeing her scars for her to be comfortable wearing clothes that revealed the damage. Her sister Jenna had given her some beautiful clothes she had handmade trying to get her to- What had Logan called it? Oh yes, let her hair down. Well, she had worn some of the things to Church, but she didn't go places that she could wear the most romantic dresses she had been given.

One of the many things that she liked and respected about Logan was the fact that he was a Christian. He opened every board meeting with prayer and there was a well-worn Bible in the private suite connected to his office where he occasionally stayed when he worked late.

Logan's strength of character was beyond that of any man she had met, except her sister's husband and her father. Longing, so strong that it left her shaken washed over her. What would it be like if she were to allow herself to lean on a man with such strength?

"Lord, in the Bible Saint Paul said that he had learned to be content in whatever state he found himself to be in. Please help me to have that same contentment." She prayed as she settled down to yet another microwave dinner to be followed by a long quiet night.

Chapter 2

Logan watched as Cassie entered data into her computer. Yes, he was right the skin on her hands, and even her neck was darker. It was at least a shade darker than her carefully applied make-up. His lips twitched as he remembered his joke about her needing some sun. She had apparently taken his advice. When, he wondered, did she find the time to sunbathe unless she was frequenting a tanning salon, too bad she hadn't also let her hair loose. Oh well, one step at a time, he was content to know she valued his personal opinion as well as professional.

She turned her head slightly and the slight scar across her cheek drew his attention. It had been one of the first things he'd noticed at her job interview and he realized that she wore the heavy make-up in an effort to disguise it. Her skills were well known and her level of professionalism was admirable.

He was happy when he discovered that she was a Christian. Not the preachy sort who tried to live your life for you, but the type you felt drawn to. He had definitely been drawn to her since the first time he'd laid eyes on her.

It had taken him two years to get her to fall into easy banter with him when they were alone. How long would it take to get her to see him as a man and not just as her employer?

'Father,' he prayed silently. 'It'll take something pretty drastic to shake her out of this comfortable rut she's settled into, but I know it's all in your hands."

If he didn't stop looking at the little curls at the base of her hairline that had escaped the confining hairpins he might do something drastic. Yes, they definitely needed something drastic to shake her out of her reserve.

Cassie could feel Logan's eyes on her, which made it difficult to concentrate on her task. Thank God for spell check. Why didn't he go to his own office? Didn't he have something else to do rather than hover over her shoulder? His nearness caused her skin to tingle and interfered with her thinking. She resisted the urge to check her hair. The scar on her scalp was covered by the heavy auburn sweep that also covered the left side of her forehead. When she could no longer stand the tension building inside her, she turned, careful not to look into his eyes.

"Is there something I can do for you Mr. Blake."

Startled he stammered, "uh, yes have you seen the new requests?"

"They are on your desk," she said pointedly.

"Was there anything you think we'd be interested in?"

"There are some good proposals you may want to see." Why was he asking her about them? Without thinking she looked up and was startled by what she saw in his eyes. For a long moment the air seemed to crackle with electricity. Then she dropped her gaze as she waited for his reply. Instead of replying, she heard a strange noise coming from him somewhere between a gasp and a cough. Glancing up she was surprised by the look of shock she saw on his face. Following his line of vision she saw what easily had to be the biggest spider she had ever seen crawling across the floor.

With a squeak of shock, she jumped up and scrambled to the top of her desk. Only when she felt strong arms about her did she realize that Logan had followed her, and if possible, looked even more panicked than she was. For just a moment she reveled in the sensations his nearness created within her, as clinging to him her emotions spun momentarily out of control. Then her practical side took over and she took a deep relaxing breath.

"Logan there's a tarantula in my office," she said in what she hoped was a calm voice. "Would you please help me catch it?"

"Catch it! Why?" The panic was subsiding in his eyes, only to be replaced by a strange light that in some ways frightened her more than the spider.

"Because we live in Boston and we don't have wild tarantulas here." She explained slowly, "It must belong to someone, and besides that, I can't see it anymore so I don't know where it is."

His arms tightened around her as he scanned the floor. He had known it would take something drastic to shake her up and this definitely fit the bill.

"Logan, let me go so I can get down and look for it." The sensation his arms created panicked her and she placed both hands against his chest and pushed just as he let her go.

Unbalanced, he staggered back a step, his foot barely catching the edge of the desk. Flailing his arms, he grabbed at her as she tried to steady him and they both toppled helplessly to the floor.

Landing on top of Logan was the last thing she wanted to do, so of course that's exactly what happened. Stunned, she lay sprawled over him her cheek resting on his firm chest, amazed that she could hear his heart pounding in rhythm with her own. A deep chuckle rumbled through him and she lifted her head in open-mouthed shock. Her wide green gaze was caught in a timeless sea of blue. Her heart fluttered into full panic as she lowered her eyes to the front of his shirt, only to be struck by the intimacy of their position.

Panic once again overcame her as she scrambled to untangle their legs. Grasping her shoulders Logan rolled her off of him. Then he jumped to his feet just in time to catch a glimpse of her long shapely legs as she struggled to push her skirt down and stand at the same time. A long, angry scar, which slashed down her right thigh, ending just above the knee caused him to catch his breath.

Recovering immediately he grabbed her hands and hauled her up, clasping her to his chest. He hadn't realized that there might be other scars than the ones on her face. The urge to comfort her for the long ago pain was too strong to resist.

"Logan," Cassie cried in embarrassment as she struggled against him.

"Sh," he murmured as he gathered her closer. "Do you see it anywhere?" he whispered with mock terror. He enjoyed the feel of her in his arms and was hoping she hadn't realized he'd seen what she'd so carefully tried to keep hidden.

"We've already made enough noise to wake the dead." Her sense of humor suddenly raised its head and light-headed laughter bubbled up from deep within her. "Help me look for it," she gasped as she swatted his arm and he reluctantly released her.

"Oh no, I'm not getting close to that thing," he smiled at her. Now, that the initial shock of seeing one of the few things that could strike terror into his heart had dimmed, he'd begun to feel quite foolish over the way he had panicked.

With mock outrage, Cassie picked up her wire wastebasket and dumped the contents onto the floor. Then, with Logan close behind they peeked around her desk.

The offending arachnid was calmly sitting underneath her chair, not moving. Slowly Logan removed the chair and in one quick movement Cassie up-ended the wastebasket over it.

"Tada! I got it." Triumphant, she turned an incredible smile on her employer.

Logan's breath caught in his throat as he gazed in stunned disbelief at the transformation.

Misinterpreting the stunned effect her smile had on him, she continued, "It's okay, I'll just call someone to take it away."

Reaching for the phone, she caught a movement out of the corner of her eye. The hall door was slowly opening.

"Terry, are you in here," a child's whisper preceded its owner into the room as a six-year-old boy slowly put his head in the door. Tousled hair, the color of a new penny, appeared first, followed by very large green eyes and a heavily freckled nose. A mischievous grin blossomed at the sight of Cassie.

"Aunt Cassie have you seen Terry my pet tarantula?"

"Evan." Cassie's mouth quirked into a wry smile. "I should have known this was your doing. Terry's under the wastebasket." Pointing behind her desk she asked, "where's your Mother?"

"She's lookin' down the hall."

Glancing at Logan she smiled, "I'll be right back."

As Cassie left to find the boy's mother he slipped around the desk and collected his pet. Logan warily took a step backward as Evan walked toward him with the Tarantula sitting calmly on his hand.

"Hi, I'm Evan," the boy smiled. "It's okay, Terry doesn't bite 'less he's scared." Holding his pet at arms length the spider gently crawled up his arm.

"That's quite a spider." Logan observed as a woman who was an almost perfect carbon copy of his assistant entered with Cassie who smiled and introduced them.

"Mr. Blake this is my sister Jennifer Thompson. Jenna this is Logan Blake."

So this is what Cassie would look like if she were to 'let her hair down' as he had suggested. The women were obviously twins. Jenna was a relaxed version of her sister wearing very little make-up, a sleeveless top and a light skirt and sandals. Her rich auburn hair spiraled around her shoulders and glinted with golden highlights, giving it a sun-kissed look. And yes, she did have a few freckles across her nose.

Handing Evan the plastic cage she was carrying, she smiled a greeting.

"It's nice to meet you Mr. Blake. I hope Evan's pet didn't cause too much trouble." Glancing around the office she noticed the trampled desk complete with crumpled paperwork and the former contents of the wastebasket strewn around the floor. She took in her sister's disheveled look and her eyes widened as they came to rest on the front of Logan's shirt.

"You know how I hate spiders," Cassie grinned.

Logan turned surprised eyes on her, realizing she was trying to shield him from looking foolish. Suddenly her appearance struck him. Her hair was clearly falling from its confines. Tendrils had begun spiraling down around her face and neck, causing an inordinate desire within him to finish the process. Her usual modest attire was rumpled and her blouse was pulled from the waistband of her skirt, which was now skewed around till the zipper was definitely in the wrong place.

Glancing down, he saw that he was also a mess. He had removed his jacket earlier and his tie had now loosened and hung at an awkward angle. His once pristine shirt was clearly smudged with a liberal amount of make-up and one shirttail was hanging out. They looked as if they had been caught in a compromising situation. Refusing to let Cassie take the blame for his phobia he sent her a heart-stopping grin.

"Call me Logan," he smiled and turned to Cassie. "I'm afraid I dislike spiders even more than you do. I'm sorry I helped you trample your desk."

Cassie smiled, "And I'm sorry I pushed you off."

Her smile made his heart jump again as it had just moments before. The skin, which now showed in patches through her missing make-up, was growing quite pink.

"I hope there won't be any bruises from your fall." She looked contrite.

"Not from *my* fall, but *yours* may be a different matter." Laughing he rubbed a hand over his chest as her face flamed.

"Surely you didn't land on top of this poor man," Jenna grinned. Looking at her sister's embarrassed face, she laughed. "You did! Oh, this is too funny. Just wait till mom and dad hear this one."

"It wasn't entirely my fault." Cassie sputtered defensively. She didn't like being caught off guard. "Logan pulled me off." Then, seeing the speculative look in her twin's eyes, at the use of her employer's first name, and heightened color in her face, she threw up her hands in frustration, and with a sigh of resignation, turned to her desk and began returning it to some semblance of order.

Logan, making sure Terry was safely back in his cage, engaged the boy in conversation, allowing Cassie some much-needed time to collect herself.

As Jenna picked up the scattered trash she glanced at her twin. There was a familiar tension between her sister and Logan. Jenna was certain that she was attracted to him. Who wouldn't be? There had been so many references lately to her employer when they got together for Sunday dinner that Jenna and her mother had wondered what was going on between them. Did Cassie know that she was in love with Logan? Jenna shook her head. She doubted it. Her twin had never done anything the easy way. Even as children, Cassie had always taken the lead in their exploits while Jenna had been content to follow along with whatever wild scheme they had embarked upon, and there had been many. Cassie's quick mind and fertile imagination had gotten them into more scrapes then she wished to remember. Evan took after her and was a constant source of wonder and exasperation.

Leaning close Jenna whispered, "Cass, if you want to tidy yourself, I'll cover for you." Smiling, she turned to the man and boy deep in conversation about the eating habits of the tarantula.

"Evan, have you got that cage fastened properly this time? I don't think everyone is as tolerant as Mr. Blake when it comes to your pet." Grinning she held Logan's attention as Cassie quietly slipped into the washroom. "I was listening for a scream as I checked down the hall-."

Closing the door on her sister's chatter. Cassie looked with horror at her reflection. The area where her make-up had come off had a definite pink line where the scar crossed her cheek. Her hair was a wreck. Most of her hairpins were lost and her clothes-. Cassie felt faint, for a moment she clutched the edge of the sink her eyes shut tightly as she fought the nausea that threatened. Surely Logan hadn't seen her scars. No, his eyes had remained friendly. There had been no revulsion on his face and he hadn't pushed her away from him.

Remembering the warm look he'd given her as he held her to him in mock terror, she didn't think he'd noticed. That thought gave her strength as she quickly repaired the damage.

Her office was empty when she returned, but her sisters' voice was coming through Logan's open door.

"Cassie was the captain of the cheerleading squad at our high school. She had no fear of heights so she was always at the top of the pyramid, and they could toss her higher than anyone else. She worked so hard getting us ready for the state championship that she lost her voice yelling and had an awful time trying to get her point across. Our faculty advisor finally had to put her in the mascot costume so she would keep quiet at the last game of the year. But even with her costume on, she still insisted on doing her jumps and throws. I think it was the first time anyone ever saw the Jasonville Tiger fly over the top of a pyramid of cheerleaders."

Laughter rang out and Cassie hurried into the room to stop more revelations from emerging.

"What are you two doing in town, besides trying to embarrass me?" She asked her smiling twin.

"There was a display at the children's museum about spiders and Evan brought Terry along to show him off. We were finished and we thought you might want to go to lunch with us."

"Can Mr. Blake go too Mom?" Evan's eyes were bright and pleading.

"You'll have to ask him yourself," Jenna smiled ignoring Cassie's pointed look.

"D'ya wanna come?" Evan turned an engaging grin on Logan.

"I'd love to and please call me Logan. I've been wanting to test drive the new radio controlled toys we are working on." Smiling at Evan he asked. "Would you help me try them out at the park?"

"Would I? You bet!" The boy's smile was beautiful to behold. "Is Aunt Cassie com'n too?"

"Sure she is pal." Logan was not letting her get out of it this time. Turning a warm smile on her he asked. "Cassie would you call research and have them send some prototypes to the main entrance? Perhaps we should leave Terry with security until we return. What do you think Evan?"

"That's a good idea. I don't want 'em to get too hot." Evan smiled.

"If you will excuse me, I'll be back in a moment." Logan smiled as he stepped into his private suite to change.

Cassie made the arrangements with research and replacing the telephone asked. "Evan would you please wait in my office. We'll be right out."

"Keep that thing in its cage or we won't be taking it home with us," his mother called after him.

Turning to her twin Cassie asked, "What exactly do you think you're doing?"

Jenna turned wide innocent eyes on her. "Just being polite. You do want me to be polite, don't you?"

"Of course I do, but don't play games with me Jen. You know what I mean. I can't get out in the sun around Logan. He doesn't need to know about my accident and how do you expect me to keep it quiet in the bright sunlight?"

"Oh Cass, what's the big deal he already thinks you're great. You're well covered and you should give Logan some credit for tact. He's not the kind of man who will treat you like a leper. You've known him for two years and you should know by now that not everyone will react the same way to a few imperfections."

"That's easy for you to say. You've never had to deal with anything worse than a pimple."

"Quit worrying, you can sit in the shade like you always do. Why can't you just enjoy yourself for a change?"

Logan ended the conversation by returning wearing a cotton shirt and khaki shorts. Looking every bit as though he was going on a happy family outing. Cassie cringed as she eyed her own attire. Oh, it was fine for the office, but the park was another matter all together.

They dropped Terry off with security and picked up the prototypes as they left the building.

After buying hot dogs from a street vendor, they headed into the park. Jenna spread the blanket she had brought under a tree and they settled down to eat.

Later, Logan and Evan 'test-drove' the remote control vehicles. Laughing uproariously as they got more and more daring, doing crazy stunts to see how the toys would hold up.

Cassie and Jenna sat watching the pair of boys, one small and the other ostensibly grown. They had a hard time trying to decide who was supposed to be the man.

"You should have had another child to keep Evan company," Cassie commented smiling.

"Oh no, with Evan one is enough. Can you just imagine what he would do to a sister?"

"I'm trying not to. His spider about scared *me* to death."

"What was all that about you and Logan falling off the desk?" Jenna asked innocently. "I didn't quite catch it."

Much to her sisters' delight, Cassie gave her an abbreviated version of what had transpired.

"Well that still doesn't explain why you two acted so guilty and looked as if you'd just gotten caught making out." She grinned as her sister choked with indignation. A lovely pink blush stole over Cassie's neck and ears. "I knew it, you're crazy about him."

"He's my boss." She said flatly. "We have a business relationship and that's all," Cassie chose not to comment on her sisters raised eyebrows, instead she changed the subject. "I can't believe I let you drag me out here. I'm burning up in this heat."

"At least you took off your jacket. I wish you would wear lighter clothes. I've given you some lovely outfits."

"I didn't think I'd need anything else when I left the house this morning. I'm in air conditioning all day and the clothes you've given me aren't appropriate for the office." She looked at her sister with an appreciative eye. "You on the other hand, always look great."

Jenna shook her head. "You can wear whatever you want and you know it. Just quit being so sensitive. You've got to be comfortable with who you are and not how you look." She eyed her sister critically a smile on her lips. "You've always been prettier than I am."

"We're identical twins you nut, we look just alike, or at least we used to." Cassie's eyes shadowed.

"Do you have any idea why you always had more friends and boyfriends than me?" Jenna rushed ahead not giving her time to answer. "It's because you had a certain quality about you a zest for living that made you a people magnet. That's how our friends could tell us apart. You were the fun one and I was the quiet one." She sighed heavily. "I know you went through a lot, but it's high time you got over it. Come on Cassie you've got to let it go and get on with your life."

For a moment Cassie sat with her gaze glued to man and boy, sadness shadowed her somber features.

"It's easy to tell someone to 'get over it.' The hard part is telling them how. Oh I know dad says to pray, and I have." Turning toward her sister her eyes begged her to understand. "I've prayed and prayed, but the scars are still there. The outward scars as well as the inner scars. God is not going to instantaneously heal me, even though he could. My miracle came the night you pulled me back from deaths door. I have to discover what God wants me to do. You tell me to get on with my life, but I don't know how." Her eyes fell to her hands clutched in her lap. Slowly she unbuttoned the cuff of her left sleeve and glancing around to make sure no one was near, she slid her sleeve up to her elbow and extended her arm to her sister palm down.

Red scars criss-crossed the back of her forearm. When she turned her palm up the ugly scar that slashed diagonally across her wrist showed.

"I tried to dress the way I wanted. I tried to ignore the stares and the comments. I just couldn't. The scars have started shrinking and pulling causing these ridges to form and this is just a small portion of the damage. My back is so marked up I could hold a chess tournament on it." She shook her head. "Someone asked me once if I had tried to commit suicide." She ran her hand along the three-inch mark on her wrist. "My own clumsy stupidity got me into this mess. I'm not blaming anyone else for what happened. The only one I have to blame is myself, not you, not mom and dad and not God. Not after all he's done for me."

There was such pain in her sister's face that Cassie reached out to her and said gently, "The only reason I'm telling you this is because I just can't 'let it go'. I can't let a man be a part of my life without showing him what a mess I am. And I can't let Logan see me like this. He deserves someone better. Someone whole."

"The girl you knew is gone. Shattered like the glass that broke in a million pieces and cut up my life and my dreams as well as my body." Her hands shook so hard she could barely fasten her sleeve back into place.

Jenna gently placed her hands over the shaking ones and carefully buttoned her sister's sleeve. Then she wrapped her arms around her twin and held her for a long moment.

"I'm so sorry. I had no idea how bad things have been for you. Every time you come around you seem so happy and I guess I just forgot that you haven't healed completely. I'll keep praying for you. Not just your body, but also your injured spirit. You've come a long way, but I can see that you still have a long way to go." Squeezing her sister's hand, she continued.

"You can't quit trying Cassie you've always been a fighter. If you feel something special for Logan, and I think you do, then you need to fight for him. Don't just roll over and play dead." Smiling she nodded toward the man and boy. "Logan isn't just some high school or college boy. I saw the way he looks at you and I have a feeling we are going to see a lot more of your boss. I have a feeling he will play a large part in your healing, body and soul."

Cassie wouldn't argue with her sister. There had been too many times when Jenna's 'feelings' had been accurate, but she wouldn't allow herself to hope for anything as far as he was concerned.

Cassie determinedly forced her feelings for Logan to the back of her mind. Jenna would never understand how she felt and she couldn't explain it herself. The last thing she wanted was for Logan to know that she felt anything personal for him at all.

Just then a very large very black remote controlled truck came up and drove in circles around them.

"Hey," Logan called, walking up with a big grin on his face and a remote control in his hands. "Things are beginning to look a little too serious over here. I came to break it up. Grab a remote and come on," he invited.

"That's okay you boys are doing just fine." Cassie demurred.

"What's the matter, aren't you up to the challenge?" The black truck sounded like it was revving its engine. Logan knew from past experience that Cassie wouldn't back down from a direct challenge.

The women raised their eyebrows at each other and scrambled to their feet.

"So you're challenging us, are you?" Cassie drawled thinking about what her sister had said and knowing that to back down now would cause a lot of undue speculation. Her old competitive spirit raised its head as she grinned.

The revving sound grew louder as Logan's grin grew wider. "I believe I am."

"You're on pal. Pass the remotes."

Jenna smiled. As she watched, the electric tension increased between the two standing before her.

Chapter 3

"Okay, we go around the pond and circle the bench twice. Then back around the pond again and across the grass. The bike path is the finish line. If your vehicle gets stuck you have to fix it yourself and anyone who hits, trips, or runs over a pedestrian is disqualified." Logan looked down the line of mismatched toys and grinned. "On your mark, get set, GO!"

Logan's black truck was first over the starting line, followed by Jenna's red sport car. Evan's police car screamed past Cassie's yellow all terrain vehicle and passed Jenna's car. Turning too sharply, the police car flipped and landed in the pond.

The yellow ATV caught up with the sport car and they raced in tandem, catching up to the black truck and following it around the bench. Where the top heavy truck rolled over twice landing back on its wheels. Logan was able to keep it upright the rest of the way by slowing down slightly.

The girl's vehicles raced side by side narrowly missing Evan who had fished his car out of the pond. It was slowly limping along, squealing annoyingly.

Logan, trying to catch up, swerved to avoid Evan's ankles and ran into the police car, sending both vehicles into the water.

As Evan cried, "No fair!" Jenna's low sport car hit a bump and went airborne nearly hitting Cassie's ATV as it raced over the finish line. Jenna's sports car bounced across the finish line in second place and came to rest against a trash can.

Laughing the twins hugged each other while jumping around excitedly.

Cassie came off the worse for wear as the rest of her hairpins deserted her. (With a little help from her sister.)

Cassie tried, unsuccessfully, to smooth her hair back into a French twist.

"Here, let me help." Jenna came to the rescue with a hair clip and a grin as she carefully arranged Cassie's mane, clipping it to one side so her scar was hidden. The clip wasn't large enough to contain all the hair, so she was 'forced' to leave it loose where it hung to her waist.

"That's better," smiled Jenna, as a light breeze lifted the spiraling tendrils, blowing them across Cassie's face.

"For who?" Cassie pretended to scowl at her sister. "I'll never get anything done today with this stuff in the way."

"Hmm, I wonder..."

"Don't even think about it."

"Well, someone has to. You obviously aren't." Jenna watched the color mount her twin's cheeks. "Or maybe you are."

"I refuse to be baited into saying something that you will undoubtedly find incriminating."

"You already have. Come on, it looks like Logan is trying to take a mud bath." Jenna grinned as arm in arm they went to watch the 'boys' retrieve their vehicles from the muddy water.

The edge of the pond was slippery and Logan was just climbing out when Cassie, throwing caution to the wind, called out, "Don't fall in!"

Looking up, he froze at the sight of his prim Assistant, her hair spiraling around her shoulders, smiling merrily at him. It was remarkable how alike the sisters were at that moment. A warm smile came over his face and he lost his footing nearly falling headlong into the muddy water. Catching his balance he reached out a hand to Cassie.

"Hey, how about some assistance from my Assistant here?"

"I don't *think* so." She smiled with a shake of her head. "You've already pulled me off a desk today and I don't want to fall into the water too.

"Oh, come on Cass," Jenna laughed. "A little water might do you some good."

"But Mom, Aunt Cassie never gets in the water." Confused, Evan glanced up from trying to shake the muddy water out of the police car. "She always sits on the deck an' watches us."

"That's because I'm the lifeguard, silly. I have to watch you." Cassie broke in before her sister could come up with a good excuse. Checking her watch she turned to Logan and exclaimed. "Oh dear, we'll never get things finished today and Monday you have to present a proposal at your meeting with the financial backers of the Farnsworth company."

Logan, who had finally managed to climb out of the pond, turned to Jenna. "Now you see why she's such a good assistant. She tries to keep me in line, even when I'm covered in mud," he grinned. "I guess we had better get going. Evan can you help me carry these wet toys?"

Cassie and Jenna gathered their things and they were soon on the way back to the office to collect Terry.

"Mom can Logan come to my birthday party next week?" Evan asked as he skipped along beside his mother.

"Now Evan, you know you are having an afternoon party. Logan has to be at work."

"Well, can he come to you an' Aunt Cassie's party on Sunday?"

"You don't have to ask my permission Evan." Jenna threw a mischievous smile to Cassie. "I'm only *your* mom. I'm not his."

"Oh yeah, sorry," turning to his Aunt he asked. "Can he come Aunt Cassie?"

With a smothered laugh at Cassie's outraged expression, Logan asked, "Can I Mom?"

"Logan! Don't be ridiculous." Turning to her nephew she explained. "Logan is my boss, Evan, I'm not his mom and he can make up his own mind."

"Well why didn't ya say so?" The boy's eyes were shining as he turned to Logan. "Do you wanna come to Mom an' Aunt Cassie's birthday party?"

"I'd love to. When is it?" Logan turned to the two women with a look of delight at Cassie's discomfort and Jenna's amusement.

"One o'clock next Sunday the eighteenth, at our parents' house in Jasonville. No gifts allowed, but you can bring your swimsuit." Jenna volunteered. "Cassie can give you directions, or better yet, you could ride up together."

"Sounds good, I don't have anything happening next weekend." Logan held the door for the women and boy as they entered the Blake International building.

After they'd collected the spider, Jenna and Evan left for home.

While Logan took the toys back to research to discuss modifications, Cassie went to her office to see if she could still get any work finished before the end of the day.

When she stepped into the washroom, she was surprised by her reflection. Her hair, which hung in soft ringlet curls around her face and shoulders, shone with rich auburn tones. Just one afternoon in the park had brought a rosy glow to her skin that two weeks at the tanning salon had not been able to accomplish. Was it seeing Logan so relaxed that made her cheeks glow? Her make-up was worn quite thin, but her scar was not very noticeable. Had Logan seen it, she wondered? Oh well, what did it matter, she shrugged? Her eyes lost some of the sparkle they had picked up over the course of the afternoon. He would never look at her as anything but his prim proper assistant anyway. It was time to put things back on a professional level. If they continued to act as they did today there was no way she could remain neutral.

Neutral? She had *never* felt neutral toward Logan. She returned to her office to find the telephone ringing. The sound brought her mind back to the normal tasks of the day. Taking a message for Logan she dug into the mountain of paperwork that had been so rudely interrupted earlier.

Ten minutes later, the door of her office opened, and she didn't need to hear the squish of Logan's shoes to know it was he. Looking up, she was surprised to find him staring at her, as if he had never seen her before.

"Excuse me." Logan stepped to the desk and picked up Cassie's nameplate. "Miss Hanson is that you?" He grinned. "Are you sure you're not her twin?"

"Evil twin perhaps," said Cassie crisply, eager to get back on an even footing, she launched into her carefully constructed speech.

"I'm sorry Mr. Blake, I want to apologize for my family's interruption. I can assure you it won't happen again." Pushing her hair over her shoulder, she avoided looking directly at him. "And, I'm afraid, I've lost my hairpins and can't put my hair up. From now on I'll carry spares with me. Though I don't foresee this happening-."

"Stop babbling woman." He sternly broke into her flow of words. "There is nothing wrong with your sister and nephew stopping by here occasionally. Meeting your family was delightful, as was today's outing. Evan helped me to discover some major design flaws in those remote controlled vehicles. Which can now be addressed."

"As for your hair," he paused as he ran a warm glance over her. "There is nothing at all wrong with it, but I can see how it could be a distraction. You may be wise to keep it confined during working hours." He paused as if he were about to say more, then turned toward his door. "I'd better change. I'm dripping all over the carpet."

Cassie sat staring at the door Logan had closed behind him. Well, It seemed he didn't want to get back on a professional level. What had he meant by her hair being a 'distraction'? It was a bit unruly, but it didn't bother her.

She caught her breath at the thought that came unbidden to her mind. He couldn't have meant a distraction to him, could he? Her heart jumped at the thought of being a 'distraction' to Logan. She tried to put a lid on her raging emotions. From now on her hair would definitely be kept up. Shaking her head, she reigned in her thoughts and once again tried to immerse herself in her work, refusing to let her mind wander to such impossible thoughts.

Logan, on the other hand, was not having *any* success shutting the door on his thoughts. As he quickly showered and changed he wondered who the real Cassie was. The competent secretary who had caught the attention of her supervisors and had quickly climbed the corporate ladder. The insightful assistant who had become an increasingly valuable part of the company or the playful, sassy woman who had beaten the pants off him in a child's game. He certainly wanted to see more of the latter.

Jenna had mentioned that Cassie was fearless in High School. He smiled at the image of her flying through the air in a tiger costume. In many ways he had seen that determination of spirit as she threw herself into her job. She often anticipated his business needs so thoroughly that he had wondered if she could read his very thoughts and sense the way that he felt whenever she was near.

Were the scars he had seen the key to the barriers she had constructed between them?

His face burned as he remembered his reaction to the spider earlier. He could have sworn for a moment, while she had leaned against him, that she hadn't minded being held by him. In fact she'd seemed to enjoy the situation as much as he had, and he most certainly had enjoyed it. Lying, flat on his back, with her sprawled across his chest, he'd had an almost uncontrollable desire to kiss her senseless. Then when he had, at last, seen her hair down- he groaned. What would she do if he walked into her office right now, locked the door and pulled her into his arms?

No! He *mustn't* think those thoughts. He *must not* think of her as a desirable woman. He *couldn't* lose control of himself now, not when he was finally starting to make some headway.

"Oh Lord," he prayed, "Help me know what to do and how to handle myself." He knew there was no way he could get through the paperwork he would need for the meeting Monday morning. Pressing the intercom, he asked Cassie to come into his office. Then he strove to act like a thirty-three-year-old businessman and not like a thirteen-year-old boy with his first serious crush.

"Yes Mr. Blake?" She looked nervous. Had he been too hard on her earlier?

"I need to leave the office. Will you be free tomorrow for a few hours so we can go over the Farnsworth proposal?"

"Certainly, what time will you need me?"

"Is eight o'clock too early?" That would give them all day if needed. And the way he was having a hard time keeping his mind on work, they would need it.

"Eight is fine with me."

He nodded. "Eight o'clock it is. I'm leaving in a few minutes and since you are giving up your Saturday morning you can leave right away if you wish."

"Thank-you. I just have a few things to finish."

Soon afterward he left the office, taking some work with him to try and occupy his mind.

Cassie sensed his mood, but couldn't understand why he had become so upset with her. Many times in the past, they had

31

switched between acting like old friends to business professionals at a moments notice. Their relationship had been on a professional basis for so long that she wondered if he was having a hard time dealing with another side of her personality. They had always had a good working relationship, whether in the boardroom or in the privacy of the office. And in one afternoon that sense of camaraderie had been blown completely away.

How, she wondered, would he react if he came to the birthday party next weekend. Her family was not exactly what could be considered conventional.

Cassie remembered how she had tried to shock her parents ten years ago at her and Jenna's seventeenth birthday. Her father was the Pastor of the local Community Church and as teenagers she and Jenna had occasionally rebelled over the restrictions he had placed over them. Cassie had been a Christian since she was a child, but sometimes the pressure of being a teenager had gotten her into trouble. That was why she had been so surprised when her parents' had allowed them to have a pool party for their birthday.

Jenna had always done what was expected of her, while Cassie had been the true rebel. After getting her parents consent for the party, she had slipped off to the local department store and bought an outrageous bikini. Knowing full well that her father wouldn't approve of it, she had waited until the party was in full swing before changing.

Emerging from her room wearing nothing but the bikini and a pair of cutoff shorts. Cassie had come face to face with her mother, who upon taking one look at her wayward daughter had asked in despair. "Oh Cassie, what in the world are you wearing?"

"My new bathing suit." Cassie said defiantly. "I like it."

Knowing she would get nowhere arguing, Melissa Hanson had looked pointedly at her daughter. "We'll talk about this later young lady, and whatever you do, *please* steer clear of your father."

Agreeing, Cassie had gone her way and enjoyed the party.

Bobby Thompson, who was home from his first year at college, had been paying a lot of attention to her this summer and today was no exception. They had laughed and joked, swimming and playing water polo. The beautiful June afternoon wore on and their guests started leaving. Cassie was out front saying goodbye to some friends, when Mrs. Matheson, her friend Sadie's mother, pulled up and asked Cassie to call her daughter.

Cassie, with her boundless energy, had run through the house looking for Sadie. Spotting her by the pool talking to Jenna and their Uncle Pete she had run through, what she thought was the open sliding glass door, it wasn't. She had crashed through the closed door shattering the glass.

The door wasn't new, and the glass wasn't safety glass. When it shattered, it came apart in large shards, which fell to the ground, splintering into millions of sharp pieces.

Cutting her left wrist a third of the way up her arm, a large shard had sliced diagonally across her face, narrowly missing her eyes. The glass had caught on her swimsuit top leaving a deep cut along her left breast. The length of her right thigh was slashed to just above the knee. As the glass crashed all around her, she had stood dumb founded, for a split second swaying, before slowly spiraling down, landing with an ear splitting shriek on her back, in the pile of broken glass.

At the sound of glass breaking everyone froze. Then as Cassie fell her Uncle Pete had raced to her side, barking orders. His years as Emergency Medical Technician stood him in good stead, but nothing could have prepared him for the horror of working on his niece.

Blood was flowing unchecked and he needed help to stem the flow immediately. Towels were brought and he assigned each wound to the many people who wanted to help. As they put pressure on the cuts to stop the bleeding they unknowingly pressed her back and the back of her left arm and legs into the broken glass under her, causing it to grind into her flesh. When Cassie started writhing in pain it caused additional damage. Quickly realizing what was taking place, Pete and the others had carried her to a chaise lounge where they were able to work without causing further damage.

The ambulance arrived as she started shivering uncontrollably. Shock had set in and Cassie slipped into blessed unconsciousness.

It had taken six hours, two teams of surgeons and five units of blood before Cassie regained consciousness. The next four days were a blur. Her Mother and Fathers anguished prayers mingled with normal hospital sounds. Infection set in and she was close to death.

In her fevered dreams she alternately argued and pleaded with God to let her die. In her mind she was on fire and in her dreams she was a monster. Through it all the prayers of hundreds of Saints who had heard of her accident whispered around and through her, soothing her soul.

At her darkest hour, she felt herself begin to slip away. Raising her hands above her head, she watched as the bandages gently fell away. Her skin cleared, and she stood amazed, clothed in a robe of pure light. Suddenly she had taken wing and was flying through the air toward the source of the light that surrounded her, toward peace and happiness, toward God. The sense of complete freedom was marred when something wrapped itself around her right hand, holding her back. She tried to pull free, but the strength of the band on her hand increased.

A gentle voice whispered through her, halting her struggles as it said, "My child, it is not yet your time. You must return and ready yourself, for you have a work to do. One day you shall help many who are hurting, even as you are now."

The light dimmed and she saw the wounds reappear. The bandages once more spiraled themselves around her bringing the searing pain with them and pulling her back to consciousness.

The sound of weeping would not stop. It accompanied the hand that held hers tightly. Slowly she forced her eyes open and saw her twin with her head on the bed clinging to her undamaged hand. Jenna was sobbing uncontrollably.

Using all the strength she possessed Cassie gently squeezed her sister's hand and when she raised her head, Cassie smiled slightly into her startled eyes, then drifted into the first peaceful sleep she'd had since the accident.

The healing process had been slow. Jenna had spent all her free time at Cassie's bedside. Bobby was also a frequent visitor, but after the look of horror the first time he saw her face, Cassie knew that their feelings for each other weren't strong enough to withstand her injuries. He continued to come even though she had told him they could only be friends.

Cassie soon came to realize that Bobby and Jenna were in love. Though they kept quiet about their feelings, Cassie had seen the growing attraction in their eyes. She watched as their relationship grew and was ecstatically happy for her twin. Bobby was a stronghold for her sister at a time when her whole world had disintegrated. There was no jealousy in Cassie's eyes as she watched them and wished she would someday find the same happiness herself.

July came and Cassie watched the Independence Day fireworks out the window of a rehab center. Slowly she regained her strength. The cut on her thigh caused her to limp slightly and she went to physical therapy for two months after she left the center.

When school started that fall, she thought she was ready, but the first day was harder than she expected it to be. Her classmates tried not to stare, but Cassie could feel their eyes upon her constantly. She had not healed sufficiently enough to wear make-up to cover her facial scars so there was nowhere to hide. The lower she felt, the higher she raised her chin. Some thought she was stuck up, while others thought she was very brave. Then came the day when she realized she had changed from the most popular girl in the school to the one most pitied and the butt of many jokes. It was not a smooth transition…

Shaking her head, she rose from her desk and went to straighten up Logan's office, determined to put that day out of her head. As she gathered the files and paperwork she noticed the door of his private rooms standing open. She had better check that he had not left muddy clothes laying around. Crossing the comfortable sitting room she entered the bedroom. Glancing around she spotted dirty clothes on the bathroom floor.

The smell of Logan's cologne assailed her nostrils as she stepped into the well-appointed bathroom. Picking up the scattered clothes she blushed as she noticed how personal dirty laundry could be.

"I was going to throw the shoes and socks out." Logan's voice startled her and she spun around, her feet becoming entangled in the offending shoes. With a cry, she lost her balance. Clinging to the counter top she dropped his clothes and stood open-mouthed clutching the edge of the sink.

"I'm sorry to startle you," he grinned. "I came back to take care of this mess. You don't have to clean up after me." As he spoke he entered the small bathroom.

Ducking her head so he wouldn't notice the color that suffused her face, she didn't see him as they both bent down reaching for the clothes at the same time. The resulting thump she received as their heads collided at the point where her scar exited her hairline. Blinding pain piercing through Cassie's head. She literally saw stars as her hand came up to her head. Staggering backward she fell into the shower stall taking the curtain with her. The curtain rod came dislodged and fell, narrowly missing Logan as he sprang to her aid.

"Hold on!" Logan called, carefully pushing the curtain to the side, he pulled her hands from her face. He gently pushed her hair back as he tried to examine her head, but she pushed him away.

"I can't see a thing! Sit still a moment." He fetched a fresh washcloth and wetting it, he proceeded, under much protest, to gently wash her face clean of the heavy make-up. A large red bump was rising where the scar disappeared into her hairline. "There, now I can see you. That bump looks pretty bad, let's get you out of here." Logan lifted her as if she were a child and carried her into the bedroom where he placed her carefully on the bed. When she tried to sit up, he placed a hand on each of her shoulders and gently pushed her back down.

"Hold still, you've got quite a bump there and you may have a concussion. I'll be right back." Ducking into the bathroom, he returned with a cold cloth and gently placed it on her forehead.

Cassie was afraid to open her eyes. She felt vulnerable without her protective mask. The last thing she wanted to see was a look of revulsion on Logan's face as he caught sight of her scars.

Though Logan had seen the slight ridge that ran across Cassie's cheek before, he had no idea how extensive the damage had been. Looking into her flushed face he once again had the desire to take her in his arms and kiss her pain away. Involuntarily he reached out and traced the crease along her cheek with his fingertip. Her eyes flew open and she was startled by the intense emotion she saw in his gaze.

"Are you okay?" He smiled at her, his fingers lingering on her cheek.

She was so pale; all color had fled her skin, leaving the scar standing out in stark relief. With a groan, she rolled away from him, burying her face in his pillow.

The bed creaked as he sat beside her. "Cassie, it's all right, I've known about your scar for a long time now. You don't have to hide from me." He spoke gently as he placed his hand on her back, rubbing absently with a soothing motion. "It's really not that noticeable." His calming words reached her even as his touch caused sparks to slide down her spine.

Suddenly Cassie stiffened. Her back…he mustn't rub her back…the ridges…

"No!"

Quickly she rolled away from him. Reaching the other side of the bed, she jumped up and turned away from him, clutching her head and swaying dizzily.

"What's wrong?" Logan was confused by her strange behavior. She acted is if she were afraid of him. Moving around to the other side of the bed he placed his hands on her shoulders and turned her to face him.

"I won't hurt you," he murmured gently.

She stood shaking with her hands over her eyes, her hair a burnished cloud around her, having finally fallen loose of its confines.

The urge to protect her overtook him. He pulled her into his arms and rocked her gently making soothing noises and stroking her hair from her face until she stopped shaking.

Placing a hand under her chin he lifted her face, his thumb sliding along her cheek. Slowly she opened her eyes and he was lost in their glistening green depths. Without thought he lowered his head and ever so gently ran his lips over the length of her scar from forehead to jaw.

Cassie was afraid to move. She must be dreaming, but no dream she had ever known could hold a candle to this. She was torn between wanting to run from him, and wanting to throw her arms around his neck and abandon all pretext of modesty.

Slowly Logan slid his hands into her hair and buried his face in the glorious spirals drawing in the scent of warmth and sunshine.

"Cassie," he breathed.

She could feel the pounding of his heart as she leaned her head against his chest. "This can't be real," she murmured her breathing ragged. "We can't do this."

Logan held her close. "No we shouldn't," he whispered in her ear. "I should go. Do you want me to leave?"

"Yes, no, I-I'm a little dizzy." She smiled as she pulled back and gazed into the depths of his eyes.

"So am I," he smiled back running a fingertip along her jaw line. "You are beautiful."

Shaking her head, she winced. "No, don't say that Logan, I know better."

Cupping her cheek in his palm he looked deeply into her eyes and saw her pain and uncertainty. "Yes-you-are," he enunciated each word so she would have no doubt what he was saying.

She smiled tentatively as she said, "I have something I need to show you." She stepped back and unbuttoned her sleeve for the second time that day. Then with a deep breath she kept her eyes on his face as she pulled her sleeve back and exposed her battered arm.

He drew his breath in sharply as he reached out and taking her scarred arm in his hands he gently ran his fingers over the ridged flesh.

"Oh Cassie, what happened?" His eyes were filled with compassion as he drew her to him. There was no revulsion on Logan's face as he asked the question.

Cassie's heart was beating heavily as, suddenly lightheaded; she released the breath she had been unconsciously holding.

"I think we'd better go and sit down where we can talk." Cassie motioned to the sitting room.

Logan urged her to sit in a comfortable chair and he took a seat near her.

Taking a deep breath she started from the beginning giving him an abbreviated version of what had happened. She told of the party, her accident, and how she had come to have the severe scarring. She skipped over the infection, the time spent in the hospital, and the subsequent surgeries to reduce the damaging effects of the scars.

Logan listened without interruption watching the play of emotions that crossed her mobile face. He was no stranger to emotional pain himself, but she had suffered in ways he could not even begin to fathom.

When she finished, he stood and drew her into his arms. He could see how much it had cost her to speak of the incident, and he figured there was much more to the story than what she was telling him. Once again, his desire to protect her came to the fore.

Deliberately, he lowered his head until his lips were within an inch from hers and holding her gaze he repeated the phrase he had spoken earlier.

"You are beautiful." His tender kiss was meant to comfort her, but when he felt her surprised response, his pulse leapt and the hunger he had felt for so long crept in unaware. He fought for control as he clutched her like he would never let her go.

Her arms unconsciously crept up around his neck and she was lost in a sea of sensation as she surrendered to his kiss.

He eased back, drawing a ragged breath. He held her to him as he tried to control the emotions that wanted to run rampant.

"Do you have any idea how long I've wanted to do that?" He asked with a sigh.

"As long as I have wanted you to?" she smiled shyly, still reeling from his touch. The light in his eyes made her blush furiously as without thought, her hands smoothed his mussed hair. The softness beneath her fingers filled her with longing and she suddenly knew that her life had irrevocably changed forever. This couldn't be happening. She had never allowed herself to even think about something like this, yet here she was abandoning all her years of pent up fear and reasoning in exchange for that one priceless kiss from Logan.

"How am I going to call you Miss. Hanson again and treat you like you are my assistant when I can't keep from kissing you?"

Her heart abruptly ground to a stop as she let her arms fall away. "I *am* your assistant." Pushing against him, she stepped back and he reluctantly released her. Carefully she pulled on her professional mask and turned away as she continued briskly. "It's who I am."

Shaking his head, he took her by the shoulders, turning her toward him as he protested.

"No, you are much more than that." Tilting her chin up, he forced her to look into his eyes as he continued. "Since you came here I've found myself looking forward to coming to work. Just having you near has made a difficult job enjoyable." He ran a hand through his hair. "I couldn't function without you here. We'll find a way to make this work."

Her heart soared as she smiled and stepped back into the informal teasing she was used to. "We can handle it, even if you are a bear with a sore head." The tension was broken and they laughed together.

"Won't you come to dinner with me?" His flashing dimples were almost her undoing.

"I don't think that would be a good idea, though I'd love to. We have an early morning and I'm not finished here yet." She was already in over her head and she needed time to think and try to sort out fantasy from reality.

"You aren't doing anything more today. That was a pretty hard whack you took on the head," he smiled ruefully. "Dad always said I was hard headed."

Cassie put a hand to the lump on her head. "Oh dear, I must look dreadful.

"Not a chance." He grinned, as she blushed crimson.

Cassie went into her office to gather her things as Logan tidied his private suite. Stepping into the washroom she once again was appalled by her reflection. She tried to tame her wild mane by twisting it up and securing it with a pencil. A quick coating of make-up covered the pallor in her face. No matter what he said, she wasn't ready to go without her mask and her co-workers would be quick to notice any difference in her appearance. When she finally appeared Logan was waiting for her with a smile.

"If you're ready Miss. Hanson, I'll walk to the garage with you."

"Certainly sir. I'm ready when you are." She grinned and saluted smartly, determined to keep the atmosphere light between them.

"We need to be careful," he chuckled, "or we'll have the entire building talking."

She shuddered at the thought of being the topic of conversation around the water cooler.

"I understand. Let's go."

Chapter 4

"There, that wasn't so bad was it?" Logan commented as he put the last folder into his briefcase. "It didn't take as long as I was afraid it would."

"Sure, it only took us all day to do three hours worth of work," Cassie commented dryly while eyeing him from across the room. Neither of them had been able to concentrate very well, even though they had tried to pretend that nothing had happened yesterday. She had resorted to humor to try and ease the embarrassment that still gripped her heart every time she thought about the uninhibited way she had responded to his kiss. "As long as we stay at least ten feet apart, we should be okay."

"But, it's no fun to stay ten feet apart." Logan grinned acknowledging their attraction. The ringing telephone stopped their silliness.

Cassie answered it with a quizzical look at Logan. It was Jenna who when she couldn't get her sister at home, had tried the office. It seemed that their parents wanted to make sure Cassie would be in Church the morning of their party.

"Don't tell me Dad is going to embarrass us again." Cassie sighed. I thought all this tenth anniversary stuff was just talk."

"You know Dad and Mom. They want us to have a big day." Jenna laughed. "I told them they should have waited for our thirtieth birthday, but they wouldn't listen."

"Heaven forbid. Tell them I'll be there at ten o'clock sharp, but I don't know about Logan."

As soon as she rang off Logan asked. "What don't you know about me?"

"A lot actually," she grinned. "My parents like doing things in a big way. They have a tenth anniversary party planned and want to make sure I'm in on everything. It starts at Church so Dad can make a big deal about his little girls." She smiled.

"Whose anniversary?"

"It's the anniversary of my accident." Cassie rushed on at the look of horror on Logan's face. "You know parents. They're trying to downplay my injuries and celebrate our lives."

"I see what you mean. Parents have a way of drawing you into things. My Father hauls me up every year and tries to auction me off to the highest bidder for his favorite charity."

"Has he gotten any takers yet?" She smiled.

"Very funny."

"Oh, that's right. Last year you sent for me to bring some proposals to the ballroom at the Hancock Hotel. The bidding went quite high as I remember." She'd had a hard time not dipping into her own savings.

"You have too good a memory sometimes," he grimaced at the memory of how forlorn she had looked standing in the shadows that night. "And for the record, the kindly Dowager who bought me for the evening talked incessantly about her dear departed husband's inventions."

"Poor little you," her voice dripped sympathy.

"So, what time are we leaving?"

"For what?" She looked confused.

"Church, you know, the place where people meet to worship God." He explained as if to a child.

"I know what Church is silly. I cut my teeth on the back of a pew...literally."

"You're just surprised that I know what it is." He dropped the banter and spoke seriously. "Cassie, we need to talk. Last night was an exception to some of the rules I placed on myself long ago. I uh, don't know what came over me, and I'd like to apologize for, well..." He broke off looking embarrassed.

Cassie blanched thinking he regretted having kissed her. She dropped her gaze for fear he would see the embarrassment in her eyes, "I'm sorry, I-"

"No don't," he broke in as he saw the effect of his words. Crossing the room he squatted in front of her chair. Taking her hand he looked into her eyes and said. "Cassie, it's not like that. I'm having a hard time keeping my hands off you," he declared ruefully. The look in his eyes as he kissed her fingers sent a lovely glow through her.

"It's going to be very hard working with you so close, but we must keep our distance for now or we may live to regret it."

The warmth of his grin brought the blood to her face and left her in no doubt what he was talking about.

Clearing her throat she nodded. "Yes, that would be wise and Logan I'm sorry, I didn't mean to misjudge you. "

Standing, he took both her hands and pulled her out of her chair "Well then, until Monday, Miss. Hanson."

"Until Monday, Mr. Blake." Smiling, she gathered the files left on the table and placed them neatly on Logan's desk. Then, with a nod she walked into her office and gathering her purse, she exercised all the control she possessed and walked out the door.

Sunday was a rough day for Cassie. She went to Church with the family, but declined lunch in an attempt to avoid questioning by her sister.

Later, when she was fed up with her own company, and she hadn't heard from Logan, she wished she had spent more time amongst the noise and confusion at her parents' house.

As the evening wore on she forced herself to take a good look at her relationship with Logan.

She had first learned about his company when Jenna had developed a product she called Caution Clings during their senior year of high school. The clings were made from a thin sheet of clear vinyl printed with colorful pictures or sayings. When they were dampened, they clung to the glass of patio doors so people would notice that the door was closed, and they wouldn't run into it as Cassie had done. Blake International recognized the potential of the product, and even though a similar product was already on the market, they had helped her develop her idea.

Cassie had been impressed by the fair way the company had dealt with her sister. The summer after college she had done an internship with them. When a position opened up she had applied for it and was hired. Now, here she was five years later wondering if she was ready to throw away all her hard work on an office romance.

She had taken more than one personal call from women who had desired to snare themselves a prize in the form of Logan Blake, and what a prize he would be. Somehow, he had always managed to keep those women at arms length with a friendly exterior.

He was even tempered, and he was normally patient unless he couldn't find what he was looking for. She had personally witnessed his compassion and generosity on more than one occasion.

And when he smiled into her eyes the world spun crazily around leaving her with the sensation that the floor had suddenly dropped from beneath her feet, and she was left suspended in a sea of blue.

There was no denying the fact that she was attracted to Logan. Just the thought of him caused her heart to flutter and her cheeks to warm. Why couldn't she be crazy about someone else she sighed?

Of course, there was danger in placing him on a pedestal. Especially when he refused to stay there. Smiling she remembered his fear of spiders. At least there was one chink in his impenetrable armor.

For years she had used him as the measuring stick against which all other men had fallen short. And now that he had kissed her, she knew with that no other man would ever measure up to him.

Dating was something she no longer indulged in. Oh, there had been many opportunities. She had gone out with a man in college. Until the night when she had explained about her accident and showed him her arm, Cassie would never forget the look of utter horror on his face. He had literally gotten sick and after that he had avoided her completely.

That put an end to the college dating game for her. Early on in her career she had briefly dated a co-worker, but she had never allowed him to get close enough to find out about her accident.

Then she had met Logan.

The first time she had seen him across a room full of her co-workers, their eyes had met, and for a fraction of a second, she'd felt an undercurrent of electricity flow between them. She wondered if he'd felt it too, as he had stood looking quizzically at her for a moment.

If she could just remain on top of her emotions, perhaps she wouldn't jeopardize her job. She would have to be careful to keep her feelings for Logan under control. She was no longer a dreamer who believed everything would turn out okay in the end. There had been too many dreams she'd had to sacrifice already and she was adult enough to recognize that Logan deserved the very best that life had to offer. There would soon come a time when he would lose interest in her and she wanted to make sure that he was comfortable enough with her to let her stay on as his assistant.

Many times in the past, she had seen people whom she thought were her friends walk away from her. She prayed earnestly that when the time came for Logan to turn away, she would be strong enough to take it. That night she spent more time than usual in prayer.

Monday morning she looked as efficient as always, but her calm expression hid her frayed nerves. She entered her office and put her things away, as she did every day. Then she entered Logan's office to check that everything was ready for his meeting. She was just turning to go when the door to Logan's sitting room opened and he came out.

"Good morning. I was wondering if you would be in early today." Logan acted normally which made it easier for Cassie to reply.

"This is the time I always arrive." She smiled tentatively. "Are you ready to meet with Mr. Farnsworth?"

"Yes, I made a few revisions last night." He launched into preparations for their meeting setting the tone for the day. As long as she avoided looking into his eyes it was easy to fall back into the familiar pattern of work. And at the end of the day they said goodbye as usual and she left the building.

The hollow sensation that had been with her all day accompanied her as she tried to eat her microwave dinner. Oh, how she longed to cook for Logan. She had spent a lot of time helping her mother in the kitchen the summers after her surgeries.

Later that evening she answered the telephone expecting Jenna and was surprised to hear Logan's voice.

"Cassie?"

"Logan? What's wrong." Concern colored her voice. Logan had only called her at home a few times on business.

"Nothing's wrong. I just wanted to hear your voice."

He wanted to hear her voice? Caught off guard she wondered what to do. Why not play along? There wasn't any harm in just talking with him was there? Her heart raced and the evening air took on a new sparkle.

"Are you still there?" From the tone of his voice Cassie knew he was smiling too.

"Yes, I'm just surprised that's all."

"I was thinking-"

"Uh oh," she grinned. "Don't hurt yourself."

"Don't be cheeky. I was thinking-"

"Yes?"

"Quit interrupting," he chuckled from deep in his chest

"Was I?"

"Yes, now let me finish."

"Be my guest," she laughed.

"You should do that more often."

"What?"

"Laugh, I like it."

"Don't change the subject. Now, you were thinking."

"I was?" Her relaxed mood was playing havoc with his thoughts. "Right. Well, I was thinking that the telephone might be a good way to get to know each other without distractions.

"That's the second time you've mentioned distractions in connection with me. I'm not so sure that's a good thing."

"Well, that depends."

"On what?"

"On if I'm trying to work," he laughed.

"Oh, I see," she teased.

"Do you? As much as I don't like spiders, I am very glad Terry came to visit."

"So am I, though I don't think I've ever been quite as embarrassed as when I landed on top of you." Her cheeks reddened at the memory.

"It wouldn't have been so bad if there hadn't been a tarantula wandering around loose." They laughed and talked for an hour.

Before hanging up he thrilled her by asking if she would pray with him.

The rest of the week passed uneventfully, as by day they remained businesslike and in the evening he would call her and they would talk for hours about everything under the sun. She found that they shared many of the same views about politics, and religion, two generally taboo subjects. They liked some of the same movies and their taste in music was similar, but mostly they simply enjoyed each other's company.

Saturday morning Jenna called a bit out of sorts.

"I've been trying to call you all week and your phones been busy. You need to either get call waiting or give me your new friend's number. Maybe they can get a message to you."

"You're a real comedian." Cassie was giving nothing away. "What's up with you?"

"Dad wants us to sing tomorrow and I can't remember all the words to 'Clothed in Light'," she sighed.

"Grab a pen. Do you remember the tune?" Cassie soothed her sister and they went over the song together.

"Thanks Cass, I'm sorry I was so grouchy." Jenna apologized. "I have a birthday present for you in the spare room at Mom and Dad's. I hope you'll like it."

"Of course I will, I always love your creations." Jenna was beginning to make a name for herself locally as a designer. With fond goodbye's they hung up the phone. Before she got three feet from the table it rang again.

This time it was Logan.

"May I speak to the best assistant in the world?" He asked playfully.

"I don't know," she laughed. "If I meet her I'll tell her you're looking for her."

"And all this time I thought it was you, even if I did have to call you *three* times before I got through."

"You aren't the only one complaining about my phone being busy." She told him about Jenna's call.

"It sounds like you need to get away from it all for awhile. How about coming for a drive with me?" This was the first time all week he had asked to see her outside of the office.

"I'd love to, What time?"

"How about now?"

"Now?" Mentally she calculated how long it would take him to get to her apartment. "Sure, I'll see you in about twenty minutes."

"No, I mean right now." Her doorbell rang. "Open the door."

"What?" Hurrying to her front door she threw it open. Logan was standing there dressed in casual khaki pants and a white cotton shirt. He grinned at her and held up his cell phone.

"Are you crazy?" She asked with a shake of her head as she turned off her phone and stood back motioning him into her tiny apartment.

'*Crazy about you,*' he thought as he stepped inside.

"Of course," he answered aloud. "You look beautiful this morning." His grin widened.

"Now I *know* you are crazy," she laughed looking down at her long sleeved T-shirt and stretch pants.

"This is the first time I've seen you in anything other than a suit," his grin was much in evidence. "I like this side of you."

There should be a law against those dimples, she thought.

"Give me ten minutes to change and I'll be ready to go." She gave him a radiant smile.

Catching his breath he conceded. "Ten minutes it is, Any longer than that and I may come looking for you."

Laughing she fled to her bedroom and reached past her suits, to the back of her closet, for the birthday gift Jenna had given her last year.

She needed something to match his mood and this was perfect. She shook out the peasant dress of lace and gauze in a watercolor print with large creamy flowers on a soft green background. Changing quickly she put on the matching full slip and let the dress fall over her head. The long sleeves were gathered at the wrists and three-inch lace spilled over her hands. The neckline was accented with lace, as was the deeply ruffled hem, which reached to her ankles. She tied the matching sash around her slim waist and stood transfixed staring at her reflection in the mirror.

That morning she had been experimenting with a new tone of make-up. She had only needed a light application thanks to her pale golden tan. Her eyes sparkled and she knew the glow surrounding her was due to far more than her tan.

Slipping her feet into narrow strapped sandals she contemplated her hair.

Pulling the clip from her ringlets she tied a narrow cream scarf like a headband to keep her hair back. Her cheeks warmed as she remembered how tenderly Logan had ran his lips over her face.

Scooping up her matching bag she placed a few necessities into it and after applying a pale coral lip-gloss, she added that too.

Smiling at her reflection, she murmured, "I *must* be crazy, but I can't help it."

Emerging from her room she found Logan standing with his back to her looking out the window. Somehow the room seemed smaller with his large frame in it. He turned and once more caught his breath at the sight of her. He started to take a step toward her then stopping himself he pushed his hands into his pockets and took a deep breath.

"Wow, You look wonderful." The light in his eyes told her all she needed to know. "Are you ready?"

She smiled and nodded not trusting herself to speak for a moment.

Logan's sleek black Lexus was the most comfortable car Cassie had ever ridden in. It put her eleven-year-old compact to shame. They drove leisurely down the coast, taking back roads that offered a spectacular view of the ocean.

For dinner they stopped at a small town on Cape Cod and found a cozy restaurant on the bay where they had fresh clam chowder, charbroiled filet of sole with a white wine sauce, lightly sautéed vegetables and crusty whole-wheat rolls.

Cassie passed on dessert, but when Logan tempted her with a bite of his cherry cheesecake, she accepted, and the sweet richness reminded her of the time they spent together. They lingered over their coffee talking and smiling and causing more than one romantic soul to sigh over them.

Logan watched in fascination as the light from the evening sun played across Cassie's animated features. She reminded him of a lovely butterfly, who had slowly emerged from its cocoon. Now she was poised, waiting for just the right wind to catch her wings and she would take flight.

For the first time since he had known her she was completely at ease with him. He was amazed that she actually believed she was unattractive.

The moment he had laid eyes on her two and a half years ago he had been thunderstruck and he still hadn't recovered. If anything, he was more attracted to her now than ever before. Her quiet reserve and calm professionalism had kept him from approaching her before, and until recently, she had rebuffed his attention. He had known it would take something drastic to make her notice him and when he was standing atop her desk he'd had a hard time letting her go.

This past week had been torture. How was he to continue pretending she wasn't becoming more precious to him each day? When every minute they were together was sweet torture and every minute apart was torment? If they hadn't spent so much time on the phone this past week he would have been more than tempted to show up at her door and-. No, he mustn't go there even in his thoughts. 'Give me strength' seemed to be the phrase most often heard in his prayers lately.

Cassie waved her hand in front of his face and snapped her fingers. "Are you falling asleep," she grinned.

"No, I'm just enjoying the scenery." His smile was warm and he left her in no doubt what scenery he was talking about.

She blushed deeply as she deliberately misunderstood him. "I love the view from here. The sun will be setting over the bay soon."

"Would you come for a walk with me?"

"I thought you'd never ask," she grinned.

Leaving the restaurant they walked down the short flight of steps to the beach where they removed their shoes and Logan rolled his pant legs up before heading for the water.

Stopping just clear of the gentle waves she took Logan's hand and facing into the wind, she spread her arms wide as the stiff breeze tugged at her dress and hair. "If you close your eyes and breathe deeply it feels as if you're flying," she told him.

Amazed that she would speak of flying so soon after his thoughts of her standing poised for flight, he followed her lead and closed his eyes. The wind blew against him and the crashing waves pounded in his ears. And with her hand tightly in his, he did feel as if he was flying and he never wanted to come back to earth.

They walked along the shore searching for shells and letting the waves roll over their feet. Laughing, they raced down the sand hand in hand like teenagers smiling as the seagulls took flight at their approach. Gathering up her skirt she flipped water at him with her foot and dashed off down the beach. He chased her across the sand and catching up to her he scooped her into his arms and spun her round until they were both breathless.

Laughing into her lovely eyes, he caught his breath as he let her slowly slide to her feet. He held her close and kissed her tenderly for the first time in a very long week. They stood wrapped in each other's arms as they watched the sun set in golden splendor.

It was a golden day from start to finish and Cassie was content to enjoy it, pushing the thoughts of possible let down firmly away. No matter what happened in the future, she would always cherish this one lovely day.

Later, when he dropped her at her door, he held her in his arms as they prayed together. Then he tenderly kissed her goodnight. Promising to pick her up at eight-thirty the next morning, so they could breakfast together before driving to Jasonville, he left.

She was still leaning against the front door smiling and wondering if it wasn't all just a wonderful dream when the telephone rang. Picking it up she wasn't surprised to hear Logan's voice.

"Miss me yet?" She could hear the smile in his words.

"Mm, a little." She teased. "I think it's your magnetic personality."

"Oh, is that it? And here I thought it was my boyish good looks."

"It could be your ever present modesty." She laughed.

"I don't care what it is as long as you miss me. Are you ready to face your family tomorrow?

"Not really," she smiled. "I wish they would make a fuss over Evan instead. His birthday is next week, but since this is the tenth anniversary of my accident Dad wants to make a big deal out of it. He thinks I've been in hiding long enough."

"I agree with him." Logan turned serious. "You are a beautiful woman and it's time you knew it."

"That's what you keep saying, but you haven't heard the comments I've heard when people don't think I'm listening," she sighed. "If I had a dollar for every time I've heard someone say 'She'd be pretty if-' Well, I'd have enough money for my next round of treatments."

"What treatments?"

"Dr. Jackson, my plastic surgeon, wants me to have laser treatments, but they are expensive. He mostly concentrated on my face when the accident first happened. I've had surgery on the most severe areas of deep scaring, but there is still so much to do. It just takes time and money."

"What about insurance? We have excellent benefits at the company."

"I know Logan, but they don't pay very well for cosmetic surgery, ' she explained patiently, "and this is no longer considered necessary."

"I'll look into it on Monday, but in the meantime I don't want you worried about it."

"I haven't worried about it since I started working for the company." She smiled. "I've actually enjoyed the time off from surgery. You've no idea how nice it is to not have six to eight weeks of recovery time every year."

"Do you really need additional treatments? Is it worth all that pain?"

Cassie was thoughtful. How could she possibly make Logan understand how important getting the treatments are to her without revealing the horrible experience she had been through so long ago?

"The treatments aren't necessary to my existence, but I feel like my life has been put on hold for too long already."

"What do you mean 'on hold'? You seemed to be enjoying life today."

"Today was an exception," she smiled thoughtfully. "It's hard to explain. When I hit that plate glass my whole world shattered. At first I just tried to get through the day with as few painkillers as possible. Then when I saw the reaction my injuries had on people I- well, I guess I just shut myself off from everyone,' she sighed. "It was easier than getting hurt. There's more than one kind of pain Logan. If you don't want to see the look in someone's eyes the first time they see the mess you've become, you just- don't look."

"Cassie, I know you've been through a lot more than anyone I've met before, but I can't possibly begin to understand why you would want to inflict more pain on yourself. I just want you to know that I'll support whatever decision you make."

"Thanks, I can't tell you what that means to me." She cleared her throat, trying to lighten up the conversation. "But, I'll remind you of your offer when I need time off."

"Oh now, you wouldn't go off and leave me with no assistant would you?" He laughed aloud.

"I'm sure I can find someone who will do a good job. Someone who's efficient and is around, oh, seventy-five, I think." She couldn't resist teasing him.

"That's no fair. I'll just have to bring our work to you."

Bring it on. Work would give me something to keep my mind busy while my body heals."

'*I can think of a few ways to keep you busy,*' he thought smiling to himself a few minutes later as he hung up his phone. He was getting in deep here and he didn't want out. Well, tomorrow he would meet the rest of her family and whether they realized it or not it would be a momentous occasion. Cassandra Hanson may not know it yet, but he wanted nothing less than to be part of the rest of her life, a very big part.

Chapter 5

The smell of bacon and coffee assailed Logan's nostrils as Cassie opened her front door. Her radiant smile momentarily robbed him of the power of speech and as he feasted his eyes upon her, he felt his heart turn over in his chest, then thump painfully.

He had no way of knowing that she had spent forty-five minutes going through her wardrobe before settling on her present attire. She had never cared much what she wore away from the office or church, as long as it covered her, but today was different.

She wore a simple royal blue blouse with a scooped neckline and long flowing sleeves. Her skirt was of the same fabric with light blue flowers sprinkled over it and a short ruffle that stopped at her knees. The outfit was a fitting background for her hair that had been encouraged to curl after her shower and which was held back from her face by a headband of rhinestones. The rhinestones were repeated in her ears as well as in the heart shaped necklace she wore and the effect was stunning.

Cassie stepped aside so Logan could enter. "Come in. Breakfast is almost ready."

Logan followed her into the kitchen where she picked up her hastily discarded apron and placed it on its hook.

"Something smells fantastic," he sniffed appreciatively. "I didn't know you could cook."

"Ah, there are a great many things you don't know about me Mr. Blake." She grinned mysteriously, as she put bread in the toaster. "How would you like your eggs," she asked, turning on the gas burner under her egg pan.

"Over medium, what can I do to help?" He asked as he removed his suit jacket.

"You can pour the coffee and there is orange juice in the fridge if you want some."

As soon as the eggs were finished she placed them on the table along with plates of hashed browned potatoes and crisp bacon. Logan, who had taken over the toast making passed her his lightly buttered contribution, and they sat down to eat.

Reaching across the table Logan took her hand and said a short prayer over their food. Such a simple act, but it struck her suddenly that she was sitting at her kitchen table praying with the man who was beginning to be more precious to her than the very air that she breathed. Quickly she blinked the tears from her eyes as she busied herself with her napkin.

"Tell me about your family," Logan urged after a moment.

"Well, Dad is the Pastor of the Jasonville Community Church and he also works part time as a caseworker for foster children in our area. There has been more than one time when he's literally brought his work home with him, because there were no foster families available. Mom and Dad are qualified for foster care, but they don't take children on a regular basis." She explained.

"That might be rather difficult since your father essentially works two jobs." Logan observed thoughtfully.

"Exactly. Mom has her hands full watching over Dad. He had a heart attack a couple of years ago."

"Nothing serious, I hope." Logan asked concerned.

"Not too bad, but enough to make him sit up and take notice. I wonder if he isn't still pushing himself too hard sometimes." Cassie poured him a second cup of coffee.

"Jenna said you were quite a handful as a girl. Was that because you were a P.K.?"

"I'm sure some of it was due to being a preachers kid, but I can't blame it all on Dad," she smiled. "There was just so much to do and I didn't always look before I'd leap." There was a rueful expression on her face as she informed him. "Our poor Mom always wanted to have a boy, but after having twins, she waited for a while to get used to us. We were such a handful that she was a bit afraid to have another child, for fear of what I'd do to him."

Logan burst out laughing and Cassie couldn't help but join him.

Working well together, they soon had the kitchen cleaned and were on their way.

Logan handled the car skillfully through the heavy traffic and in no time, they were heading south on interstate ninety-five. Cassie sat quietly, waiting until they were out of traffic before starting a conversation.

"We're making good time."

"Let me know which exit to take before we get there."

"You don't want me to spring it on you at the last minute? I've noticed you don't like surprises."

"I don't like *some* surprises. I do like living on the edge sometimes, I just don't like taking chance's with someone's life."

"That's one of the things I admire most about you. 'Safety First' has always been your motto."

"You can never be too careful. I was thinking..."

"Oh no, not while you're driving."

"Don't be cheeky," he grinned.

"I wouldn't think of it," Cassie smiled demurely.

"Okay, okay I give up." Logan laughed. "I was thinking that if there had been Caution Clings on your patio door you probably wouldn't have had your accident."

"Caution Clings are a great invention. They're colorful, cute, and easy to use, but they weren't invented until after my accident." Grinning at his surprised look she continued. "The inventor was a high school senior at the time, and is still receiving royalties from those adorable little stickers."

Surprised that she was so knowledgeable about the product, he asked. "Do you keep track of all the inventions we develop?"

"Not all of them, but this particular invention was made by my twin sister."

"Jenna? You're kidding," he shook his head laughing. "I should have known Jennifer Hanson was your sister."

"How could you? She's not Jennifer Hanson anymore. I introduced her as Jenna Thompson."

"Any more skeletons in your closet?"

"Well, not skeletons exactly." She paused biting her bottom lip and he glanced in her direction,

"Spit it out," he grinned.

"Well it's just that I don't think Mom and Dad are going to believe that you only came because Evan invited you."

"Hmm, the old, 'What are your intentions toward my daughter?' routine."

"Maybe not quite that blunt, but yeah, something like that, "She grinned embarrassed. "I wanted to warn you so you can get your 'We're just friends' speech warmed up."

"So, that's our story?"

"Officially-yes."

"Well, who am I to argue with a beautiful woman?" Grinning at the sweep of color in her cheeks he asked, "is this our exit coming up?"

"Yes it is. Turn right at the stoplight." She continued giving him directions and soon they were pulling into the Church parking lot.

Taking a deep breath she reached for the door handle. Logan, sensing her nervousness, took her hand and gave it a reassuring squeeze.

"It'll be okay, these are the same people you see every week, not strangers."

"Yeah well, strangers might be easier to deal with," she grinned, her spirits buoyed by the warmth of his smile.

Friends Cassie had known for years waved to her as she and Logan took their seats beside her Mother.

Melissa Hanson gave Logan a warm smile as her daughter quietly introduced them. Sharing a songbook with Cassie, Logan joined his rich baritone with the congregation, singing the old hymns they had grown up with. By the time her Father walked to the podium Cassie was feeling much more relaxed.

"Good morning everyone. As you all know I have been blessed with two beautiful daughters who have given me much joy and gray hair." He beamed as he listened to the chuckles from the congregation.

"Today we are celebrating their twenty-seventh birthday. It doesn't seem possible that twenty-seven years could have slipped by so quickly. As a favor to me I've asked them to sing this morning. Come on up here girls."

Walking to the platform Jenna and Cassie clasped hands as had been their habit since children. Jenna sensing her sister's nervousness gave Cassie's hand a reassuring squeeze.

From the time they were old enough to sing 'This Little Light of Mine' their father had stood them before the congregation. Both girls had taken piano lessons at an early age and when Cassie needed therapy to increase mobility in the fingers of her left hand, she had spent long hours at the piano.

The experience she'd had when she'd been so close to death had left her with a desire to share what had happened with the people around her, and she had written the song 'Clothed in Light'.

Seated at the piano she drew a deep calming breath and placed her fingers upon the keys. Shutting out her surroundings, her mind went back to that night ten years before. The same sensation washed over her again and she started to sing. Her soft contralto leading the way and Jenna's voice, so much like her own, joined her in harmony. Jonathan Hanson's message that morning was centered on near death experiences. No names were mentioned as he contrasted the difference between the experiences of a few people he had either read about or spoken with. To some their brush with death had been terrifying and to others peaceful. As his message drew to a close he asked the questions uppermost on his mind.

"When the time for your death draws near will you be ready to go, or will you plead for another chance to do the things God has appointed for you? Will your heart rejoice in the light or will you descend into darkness? Now is the time to think on these things. Your life can change in the twinkling of an eye, never to be the same again. You must open yourself to the Light of God's love. Shall we pray?"

The invitation for those to come to the altar for prayer was given and many that day made their way into the light of grace.

As they left the Church, Logan stopped for a moment to speak with Cassie's father as she walked over to speak with her Mother and Sister.

"I enjoyed your sermon this morning," Logan said seriously. "Sometime, I'd like to meet someone who's had a near death experience."

"You already have," Reverend Hanson smiled as he nodded toward Cassie. "My daughter wrote the song she was singing today after she nearly died. You should ask her about it sometime."

"Thank you I will."

"I'll be just a little longer here, but I'll see you at the house. I hope you brought your swimming gear."

"Does Cassie swim?" Logan asked, looking toward Cassie. Evan had mentioned that Cassie never got in the water and from what he had seen, he guessed that she wouldn't welcome a swimsuit.

"No, not any more." Following Logan's gaze, Reverend Hanson shook his head sadly. "I haven't seen her swim since the accident, she used to be quite the mermaid. She was on the swim team and was a lifeguard at the local pool." Sighing heavily he pulled a rueful smile. "A lot of things changed that day ten years ago. It's strange how something as simple as passing through a door can change lives so drastically."

There had been a tension building within Cassie that had started during her father's sermon. Sensing the change in the conversation behind her, she left her Mother's side and tucking a hand in her Father's arm asked with a smile. "Why are you two looking so serious?"

"Logan was just asking about near death experiences and I advised him to talk you about yours."

"I see," her smile froze. "Anything specific you want to know?"

Logan could see she didn't want to talk about it right then so he said simply. "Later perhaps. Right now I think we have a party on our hands."

Turning to the elder Hanson's he asked. "Would you mind my taking the birthday girl away for a little while? We won't be long"

"Not at all," smiled Cassie's Father as they shook hands again. "We'll see you when you get to the house."

Waving goodbye Logan drove to a nearby park they had passed on their way to the Church. Stopping the car he turned toward Cassie and asked. "Are you okay? You seem on edge."

Seeing the concern in his eyes she smiled absently and turned away. "I'll be fine, I'm used to it."

"Used to what?" When she didn't answer he turned her face toward him and urged, "Cassie, what's wrong? I've never seen you so ill at ease. We've been in some pretty sticky situations in the boardroom and you've never shown any sign of nervousness. Now you're wound up tighter than an eight day clock and I'm afraid that if you don't unwind a little you're going to explode."

"I can't-" she squeezed her hands together and sighed. "You wouldn't understand."

For a moment they sat quietly then Logan took a deep breath and started to speak.

"I'm going to tell you something I haven't told anyone. When my mother died Dad was a mess. He felt her death was somehow his fault. You see he was there when she died. For months we worried that he might take his own life and he was kept under constant watch. The business fell to me and I was in so far over my head that I was scared witless. If I hadn't worked for the company during college and after I graduated I wouldn't have been able to pull it off. As it was I had a lot of help from the senior officers." He took her hand in his as he continued.

"One of the hardest things I had to deal with was the well meaning people who kept watching me and wondering what I felt, and if I was handling everything okay. I wanted to yell at them to get out of my face and leave me alone." Grinning ruefully he confessed, "I'm afraid I lost it one day with Charlie Parker. He was trying to get me to lighten up on safety testing and I blew my top."

"Oh, Logan! I'm so sorry." Cassie cried. "I knew there was something between you and Charlie, but I didn't know what it was. That's why you always have an alternate proposal for him."

"I have a lot of respect for him, he keeps me on my toes concerning many of the aspects of business I might otherwise let slide."

"Why didn't your father step back into the company?"

"He tried to about a year after the accident, but he just couldn't make himself continue. He hasn't sat idle though. Many of the inventions we've developed were made possible because of the research and testing he does in his own home. He develops the testing procedures and equipment needed to insure the safety of our workers."

"I knew he was involved with testing, but I had no idea how."

"He doesn't want recognition. He's content to work behind the scenes. Right now he's working on a project with a friend from his club." Squeezing her hand he continued.

"We have both known pain in different forms Cassie. The day I blew up at Charlie was both the worst and the best day of my life. I felt terrible, I hid out in my private suite fuming and railing at God for dumping all of this on me. At the age of twenty-two I knew I wasn't ready for the responsibility of running a multi-national company. I'm afraid I wasn't as mature as I thought I was. When I calmed down I realized it wasn't Gods fault that my mother died. She was a Christian and had taught me to believe in God from the time I was a baby, but I never really knew Him. That's when I gave my heart and soul to God. I met Him that day and I can't begin to tell you the difference it's made in my life."

"Your experience was miraculous to say the least. You physically saw the light that I'm trying to follow. The light my mother now lives in, and that's an incredible thing."

The look of awe on Logan's face gave Cassie's heart wings. Many had asked her about what had happened the night she had nearly died out of morbid curiosity either questioning or cheapening her experience. She had learned to keep quiet about that aspect of her life. At first she had been afraid of Logan's reaction to her story, but now she desired to share with him one of the most deeply spiritual experiences of her life.

Carefully she recounted to him everything she could remember ending with, "I don't know what God has for me to do, I only know that with all my heart I want to do his will and if that means taking my life off hold I'm ready to do it. I just wish I knew how," she grinned.

"Well, your life has seemed to be very active all week." Cupping her face in the palm of his hand he asked. "Are you ready to dazzle your family?"

"Dazzle?"

"Yes dazzle. Just let your smile out and everyone will know that you're alive and well."

A bubble of laughter escaped her causing her eyes to twinkle and an unaffected smile to break across her face. "If I go mooning about with a goofy smile plastered on my face it's going to make everyone jump to conclusions."

Logan's dimples deepened. "Now that's the smile I was talking about. There's nothing goofy about it. Let them jump to whatever conclusions they want, as long as you don't start wearing your polite look."

'Oh Logan,' she thought. 'I don't think I could get through this without you.'

The look in her eyes made his heart jump and when he lowered his head she met him halfway in a tender kiss.

He held her for a moment before putting her firmly away from him. His smile matched her own bemused expression as he started the car. "If we don't get going we'll miss the party altogether."

"We aren't late. The party doesn't officially start until one." Continuing to smile she gave directions to her parent's home.

"Mom and Jenna will have everything set up for the barbecue by the time we get there. You should probably park here. I doubt you could get any closer."

Logan caught Cassie's hand as she reached for the door handle. "Have I told you today how beautiful you look?" he asked, pressing his lips to her hand.

"Have I told you what incredible eyes you have?" She countered his question with a question. Laughter broke out as they both blushed furiously.

"Okay, Truce?" He asked grinning.

"Truce," she conceded.

Catching Logan's hand as he reached for the door Cassie boldly cupped his cheek and rubbed her thumb across his bottom lip. "You had a little lip-gloss on your mouth," she said huskily.

Clearing his throat he gave her a quick kiss. "I'm beginning to like lip-gloss." He smiled.

They were still grinning as Cassie led Logan to the front door of her parent's home.

Jenna who must have been watching for them opened the door at their approach. She wore a stunning ensemble consisting of a slim fitting golden top made of a soft stretch fabric. The long right sleeve went to her wrist, but her left arm and shoulder were bare, save for a thin matching string that tied at her left shoulder, keeping her back well covered. The skirt had a sheer fabric overlay printed with exotic flowers, over a background of the same golden color as the top. It was the perfect foil for her hair, which was worn in a headband like her sister's.

"Wow, you look great!" called Cassie.

"There you are." Jenna blushed. "Logan, come in and meet my husband." Jenna ushered them into the living room and beckoned to a tall blonde well built man standing near the window.

"Bob, this is Cassie's friend Logan Blake. Logan, my husband, Bob Thompson." As the men shook hands Jenna continued, "Would you mind if Cassie and I run off for a few minutes?"

"Take off," Bob waved them away and turned to Logan. "I thought twins were supposed to have ESP or something. Those two always have their heads together."

Jenna pulled a face at him as she urged her sister from the room. "Come on, I have something for you."

Entering the guestroom where Cassie occasionally slept when she stayed for the weekend, she stopped and gasped. Hanging on the closet door was a replica of the outfit Jenna was wearing. "Oh Jen, it's beautiful."

"Yours is a mirror image of mine so your left arm will be covered and I made sure your back won't be exposed." Jenna's voice grew stern. "Don't say no! I think Logan will like it. She rolled her eyes. That mans' dimples are lethal, they should come with a warning and his eyes-Wow. You need to knock his socks off!

"What happened to my sweet quiet sister? I wasn't going to argue with you. I-I think his socks could use a little knocking off." Blushing, she grinned delightedly at her sister's face as her cheeks took on a rosy glow.

"Is Logan the one you've been on the phone with every evening?" Jenna started putting two and two together as she helped her sister change.

"We have been talking some." Cassie avoided wishing her color would cooperate.

"Praise God for Evan's spider." Jenna breathed fervently as she straightened Cassie's skirt and adjusted the tie at her shoulder. "Have you told him about the accident?"

"Yes, I showed him my arm and explained to him what happened the same day you were there." Her color deepened as she remembered Logan's reaction upon seeing the scarring.

"Well, that must have been quite a talk." Jenna grinned taking the dreamy look on her sister's face. Their eyes met in the mirror as they took one last look. Jenna thought their happy smiles were almost identical. "That man won't have any socks left by the time we get done with him. Just make certain he knows which arm is bare. I don't want to be embarrassed by having your boyfriend's arms around me again."

"It's a good thing it happened or you might not be a happily married woman today" Cassie grinned as she pulled a package from her purse. "Happy birthday Jen."

Jenna ripped the paper from the package and exclaimed over the silver picture frame and the gift certificate from a top notch Boston photographer.

"Oh Cassie, you shouldn't have. It's too much." Jenna protested.

"Just don't forget to save me a picture." Cassie admonished as she linked her arm with her sister. "Now aren't we supposed to do some 'sock knocking' or something?"

Laughing they went in search of their men.

* * *

Logan found Bob Thompson to be an interesting companion. He introduced him to many friends and relatives meanwhile keeping up a string of anecdotes about the girls that kept a constant smile on Logan's face.

"I wish I'd known them when they were young. They sound like they were a lot of fun to be around." Logan laughed after a particularly funny story.

"Sometimes it got very confusing. I dated Cassie for awhile the summer of her accident. It was at the birthday party ten years ago when I slipped up behind her and gave her a big hug. She took a swing at me and I was so surprised that I sidestepped and fell into the pool dragging her in with me." He shot a sideways grin at Logan letting him know that he'd heard about the desktop incident.

Logan laughed as Bob continued.

"Imagine how I felt when I surfaced with a lovely mermaid in my arms only to discover that she was Jenna." His features held a bemused expression as he ran his hand through his blonde hair. "My life was never the same again after that."

During the ensuing laughter the girls made their appearance arm in arm.

"Oh my goodness," Bob gasped. "Which one is which?"

Logan who had temporarily lost the power of speech walked to Cassie taking her hands in his. Finding his voice he smiled.

"There you are Cassie. Your mother's been looking for you." The commonplace words were delivered with a look that had Cassie blushing again. They completely missed the smiles that passed through the crowd.

As Logan and Cassie wandered off to find her mother, Bob put his arm around his wife.

"Now tell me again the difference in your clothes," He teased half-seriously. "Cassie looks happier than I've seen her in ten years and I'm not so sure I can tell the difference between you two."

"Her right arm is bare and my left one is. Just remember that it was my right arm that was scarred and I'll let you live." Jenna grinned up at him.

"Watch it or you'll end up in the pool again."

Their lighthearted banter continued as they went to help with the food.

Bob was the barbecue chef. Wearing a large apron and brandishing his long handled tools, he somehow managed to deliver mouth-watering ribs, hamburgers and Evan's favorite food, hot dogs.

Two long tables groaned under the weight of succulent baked beans, potato salad, garden salad, fresh fruit and a host of other dishes. The chilled watermelon was on the dessert table with the birthday cake. Two ice-cream freezers were busily churning in the background, while Sadie's husband, Jim Wheeler, tended them with the help of their two-year-old son Jimmy.

After their lunch had a chance to digest, Evan and a few of his friends took advantage of the pool. Cassie was happy in her capacity as lifeguard. She and her Uncle Pete had their work cut out for them, keeping the kids from getting too wild. Evan had told and retold the story of their afternoon in the park until, by now it was a legend.

Sadie's daughter, five-year-old Susan, asked shyly if Miss. Cassie would show her how to run a remote control car some day. Cassie smiled ok and assured the little girl, who was a replica of her mother, that if she were to get one, Cassie would be happy to show her how to run it. With a smile, Susan skipped off to tell her friends of her good fortune.

Cassie was summoned into the house to greet a guest and left her Uncle Pete in charge of the pool. Walking into the living room she was happy to see a distinguished gentleman in his early fifties seated near her Father.

Dr. Ted Jackson had become a good friend of the family and always enjoyed his visits with the Reverend, as well as the rest of the family. At the sight of Cassie the Doctor rose and took her extended hands.

"Cassandra my dear, let me look at you." He ran his eyes over her professionally. "Ah, very nice. I see you finally started getting a little sun, and is this happiness I see in your eyes?"

Cassie tried to remain calm, but the betraying color would creep into her cheeks. Smiling she used the phrase he had used on her many times. "How can one fail to be happy on such a beautiful day?"

"Very good, you are learning." He smiled and asked, "Is there somewhere we can get away from the crowd. I'd like to speak with you privately.

"You can use my office," offered her father.

"Excellent. Just don't go too far my friend there is something I'd like to discuss with you and your dear wife."

Cassie led the doctor to her father's small office and offered him a seat.

"So young lady, how have you been?"

"Very well thank you, I've been tanning some and the scars aren't as noticeable as they once were. The last round of work healed well and the redness is almost gone."

"As it should be. Do you realize it's been three years since your last treatment?"

"I know it's been a long time and I should either get used to how I look or resume treatments. I will not go into debt over this." Cassie recited her reason for waiting. "I've almost saved the money needed to start the new round of laser therapy and I'll call the office when I'm ready."

'May I examine you?" He smiled as she nodded resignedly. "Good, I'll call your mother."

Cassie's mother, who had been waiting with her husband, stepped into the room.

"I had an idea you might need me," she smiled.

After a brief examination of Cassie's scars, the Doctor asked Rev. Hanson to join them. The room was small and he leaned against the open door jamb as the Doctor addressed them all.

"I may have a solution to this stubborn young woman's financial problems. There is a different procedure we can try. I've developed a new laser technology that seems to do a much better job of erasing unwanted scarring. Cassie would be a perfect candidate as her scarring is quite varied. There would be no charge for the procedure, if she consents to be my test subject.

"No!" Logan, who was looking for Cassie, had approached the small group just in time to hear the end of the proposal.

In the shocked silence that followed his cry, Logan's eyes bored into Cassie's. All color had drained from his face and as she watched she saw a curious mixture of pain and fear play across his features.

"Logan, what's wrong?" Cassie stepped toward him through the crowded room.

"I won't let anyone use anything experimental on you." The pain she had seen in his eyes was back in full force.

Cassie held the hands Logan extended to her. "Dr. Jackson wouldn't do anything to put me in danger."

Oblivious to all but each other they stood holding hands. Logan was trying to control the panic that rose up at the mention of an experimental procedure. A muscle twitching in his cheek gave away his tension.

"You can't tell me that you are actually considering letting someone experiment on you." His shock was evident. "Not after all the times you've gone to bat with me to insure safety testing."

Before Cassie could speak Dr. Jackson stepped forward.

"Cassandra is this the young man who is responsible for this new sparkle in your eyes?"

Cassie made the introductions in a strained voice as Logan fought to regain his composure.

"Logan Blake, of Blake International?" The Doctor asked grinning widely. "Well, my boy. Theo has told me all about how well you've done with the company. Your father is as big a stickler about safety as you are." He reached out to shake Logan's hand.

Logan placed his arm around Cassie and pulled her to his side in an unconsciously protective gesture as he shook hands with the Doctor. "You know my father?"

"Oh my, yes. We attend the same club in the city and when I mentioned the equipment I've been working on, he started asking questions. We've been working together on it ever since," he grinned.

"You see Logan, your father and Dr. Jackson aren't going to test an untried piece of equipment on anyone." Cassie smiled encouragingly up at him, and laid her hand against his chest. She could feel his heart beating heavily beneath her palm.

Logan scanned the face of Rev. Hanson who, with his arm around his wife was grinning delightedly. Running a hand through his hair he smiled sheepishly.

"I'm afraid I overreacted a bit. I'm sorry, but-"

"No harm done, I understand," the doctor broke in quietly. "Theo will be happy to hear we've met. I intended to ask Cassandra to make me an appointment with you. I wanted to send in a proposal, but Theo wanted to speak directly with you."

"As soon as I get to the office tomorrow I'll take care of it," Cassie smiled.

"So this is where everyone has gotten to." Jenna's voice was about the only thing that could fit in the small room. "Hi Dr. Jackson, what's going on?" She asked as the doctor and her Parents headed for the living room.

"I was just telling your family about a new breakthrough I've been working on." Dr Jackson's voice faded as Logan shut the office door effectively closing them in and the rest of the family out.

"I owe you an apology," he began.

"No Logan, you don't have to explain."

"Yes, I do. I need you to understand why I panicked." Motioning to a chair he smiled, "sit down. I want you to hear me out."

Taking a seat he turned his tortured gaze upon her and ran his hand through his already rumpled hair, in the endearingly familiar gesture that showed his nervousness.

"I don't like poorly tested equipment because it was an untried piece of machinery that killed my mother." Cassie drew in a sharp breath as he continued. "She was in research and development working on a completely different project. For some reason she had come into the area where they were testing an untried piece of equipment without her protective gear in place. When the hydraulics unit exploded the three other people who were working on it were injured including my father. Mom wasn't so lucky, she died a few hours later."

While he was speaking Cassie had slipped to her knees before him. Tears filled her eyes as she once again placed her palm against his heart, trying to still the pain he was feeling. He pulled her to him holding her fiercely for a moment before relaxing his hold on her allowing her to breathe.

"I can't take chances with you're life Cass, you're too precious." He rubbed his slightly abrasive cheek against hers.

"I'm so sorry about your mother Logan. I know we joke about being crazy, but I'm not so crazy as to try something that may injure me or someone else."

"I realize that, but I was caught off guard when I walked up and overheard something about you having an experimental procedure."

"You're just worried that you won't be able to find another assistant who hides your files as well as I do." She teased a smile back into his eyes.

"I think we blew our 'just good friends' story," he said ruefully.

"*We* nothing mister," she grinned. "*You* blew it."

"Oh well," he rested his forehead against hers. "At least your family won't be surprised to hear that we're dating." He kissed the end of her nose.

"Are we?" she asked with a smile. "Dating I mean. It's been so long since I've dated that I think I've forgotten how."

"I could sign you up for a refresher course," he smiled. "We could skip over the awkward part since we've already progressed to sharing lipgloss."

Keeping her eyes on his lips, she felt a familiar warmth begin stealing through her threatening to turn her bones to mush.

"How is it that I can feel terrible one moment and the next I feel as if the sun has finally come out?" she asked breathlessly as he drew her closer.

"It's my magnetic personality."

"And all this time, I thought it was your boyish good looks."

Their lips met gently and then even as he wanted to deepen the kiss and get lost in her sweetness, he eased back.

Burying her head in his shoulder she breathed deeply, trying to calm the turbulent emotions that threatened to run wild every time he came near her.

"I think we have the lipgloss thing down pretty well." His voice rumbled in his chest as he chuckled.

Lifting her head she smiled. "I've always been a fast learner."

"We'd better get going before we are invaded by a certain spider loving boy." Logan laughed, releasing her so she could stand

Evans voice was heard clearly calling, "Where's Aunt Cassie, The ice cream's ready."

Grinning, Cassie took Logan's hand as they headed toward Evan's voice."

"Did some one mention ice-cream?" Cassic called as she walked outside through the same doorway that had changed her life so long ago.

"Come on Aunt Cassie, we need ta light the candles." Evan called as he pulled Cassie to the head of the table.

Taking her place next to Jenna, Cassie hugged her sister tightly. Ten years ago they hadn't gotten to this point when the party had taken a turn for the worse. Then the candles were lit and everyone began to sing.

Standing hand in hand with her twin, Cassie scanned the faces in the crowd. Many of the same people who were at the party ten years ago were here today. Sadie stood with Jim and their children, Susan and Jimmy. Uncle Pete and Aunt Kathy held hands as Pete gave the girls the thumbs up sign. Their son William was in the Army and couldn't be there, but he had sent his love. Her father held her mother as with tears in their eyes they tried to sing. Bob stood with one hand on Evan and the other on Logan's shoulder, in a show of support.

There were many more friends and relatives, but when her eyes met Logan's everyone else faded into the background. For an eternity that lasted but a split second, they were the only two people in the world as a bond as fine as a silk thread pulled at their hearts. Weaving them together. Healing their wounds and binding their souls.

Jenna pulled her back into her embrace. Looking into her sister's face, Cassie irrefutably knew that for the first time in a decade, she was totally and completely alive.

Jenna wiped away her tears as she saw the release she had longed to find in her twin's eyes.

Holding hands they took a deep breath and blew out the candles.

Laughing and crying at the same time their loved ones surged forward to embrace them.

Logan waited until the crowd had thinned. Then he quietly slipped his arm around Cassie's waist and when she looked up at him with radiant eyes he kissed her soundly much to everyone's delight. Smiling into her shining eyes he whispered.

"Happy Birthday."

Chapter 6

Logan stretched his arms above his head as he watched Cassie and Jenna place the last bag of trash in the can. He felt like a heel not helping, but every time he even had tried to get near, he had been told by one or more woman to go relax.

"The only time I get out of cleanup duty is when all three 'Hanson women' are involved." Bob grinned. "It's nice to pretend I'm a man of leisure for a change."

Bob addressed the sleek wet head of his son. "Okay, Evan it's time to dry off and get changed."

"Aw Dad, do I have ta?" whined Evan, even the freckles sprinkling his snub nose begged for more time.

"Yes you have ta," grinned Bob. Then he softened slightly. "Okay one more cannon ball then it's off to change with you."

"Yippee!" Evan cried as he climbed out of the pool.

The men laughed as Evan tried to make his biggest splash yet. Then he climbed the ladder and grabbing his towel hanging from the deck rail he headed in to change.

"You have a great boy there." Logan smiled as he watched Evan go.

"Thanks. He's a lot like his Aunt." Bob glanced at Logan. "Are you planning to ever have a family?"

Logan grinned, "I'm working on it."

"Sorry to be so nosy, but I worry about her." Bob glanced over at Cassie as she wiped the tables down laughing at something

81

Jenna was saying. "I don't want to see her get hurt any more than she already has."

"The last thing I want to do is hurt her." Logan kept his eyes on Cassie as he reassured him. "She's too precious."

Bob, who had been watching Logan's face as he spoke cleared his throat. "Thanks."

Changing the subject Logan said. "I hope you don't mind, but I brought an early birthday gift for Evan."

"You didn't have to do that, but I'm sure he will be thrilled." Bob smiled as Cassie and Jenna, trailed by their parents walked toward them carrying a tray of iced tea. "You three girls make a great team,"

Standing, the men brought extra chairs for the twins and their parents who approached holding hands.

"If you will excuse me for a moment, I'll be right back." Cassie turned puzzled eyes on Logan as he left through the gate to the front of the house.

"So, you two are an item," Bob stated boldly. "Hey," he protested as Jenna elbowed him. "I didn't say anything wrong."

"You don't have to tell us anything." Jenna assured her sister as she sent her husband an apologetic glance.

"I'm not sure there's anything to tell," Cassie hedged. "We're just good friends."

Cassie's father choked on his iced tea as he joined the laughter. "That's not how it looked from here. I thought for a moment that he was going to draw his sword and defend you from the evil Dr. Jackson." The group laughed. Privately he felt the two of them resembled a ticking time bomb. Both were a bundle of pent up emotions, but he was mostly worried about his daughter. He smiled as Cassie blushed furiously confirming his suspicions. He mentally added this new request to his already burgeoning prayer list.

"Okay, we just started dating, but that's all so don't read anything into it," she admitted.

"I don't see how you get any work done with all the going's on Jenna's told me about." Her mother smiled as she took in her daughter's heightened color.

"What did you tell them?" Cassie turned aggrieved eyes on her twin.

"Just that I caught you two in what appeared to be a compromising situation." Chuckling at her sister's outraged expression, she continued. "There they were, Cass looked as if she'd just been mauled by a bear and Logan looked as if he'd been caught with his hand in the cookie jar." Shaking her head she continued, "it was so funny when the situation dawned on them."

"Well I for one am glad it happened. You deserve happiness Cassie." Bob raised his glass in a salute to her.

"We're all happy for you honey." Her mother raised her glass with the rest of them as they drank a 'toast' to Cassie's happiness.

Logan returned carrying duplicates of the large black remote controlled truck and the police car they had tested the previous week. Both vehicles were new and shining with a big red ribbon on each.

Evan chose that moment to walk out of the house. Spotting the toys he gave a loud whoop and ran to Logan.

"Wow! Are those for Mom an' Aunt Cassie?" he asked eyes beaming.

"No pal, They're your early birthday present."

Evan's eyes grew as round as saucers, then they crinkled in delight. *"I get both of 'em?"*

"I thought it would be more fun if you had two. Now you and your dad can both play." Logan explained as he placed the toys on the ground and handed Evan the remotes. "We worked the 'bugs' out of them. The police car turns easier and we lowered the center of gravity on the truck."

Bob joined them and Evan carefully explained to his Father how to operate them. Bobs' eyes were tender as he watched his son acting so responsibly.

"Remember now, they run better, but they still aren't waterproof." Logan smiled as he sat down next to Cassie.

"Thank you Logan, that was very thoughtful." Jenna laughed as Evan cautioned his father to be careful.

"These are poto-tikes Dad, there ain't any others like 'em."

"That's *prototypes* Evan," his father corrected him. "Your pronunciation leaves something to be desired." Chuckling, the man and boy steered the toys into the front yard to try them out on the quiet street.

Rev. Hanson sighed contentedly. "This has been a wonderful day, it feels great to relax."

"You work too hard Dad," Cassie commented. "I'm glad you canceled the evening Church service.

"That's something I haven't done in quite awhile, but considering the fact that we've just spent all day with half the town, I think it was a wise move."

"We did have a good turn out. I've always liked having a large gathering of friends over." Melissa smiled at her daughters, "thanks for helping."

They chatted comfortably for a few more minutes before Bob and Evan returned.

Evan walked up to Logan and in his most grown up manner extended his hand. "Thank you again for the truck and car. I'll take real good care of 'em."

"You're welcome, Evan. I knew I could trust you." Logan gave the boy a conspiratorial wink as he shook his hand.

"If you're about ready to go Jenna we'd better get this fella home." Bob grinned, while tousling Evan's hair.

"We'd probably better get on the road too, if you're ready." Logan suggested, as he stood offering his hand to Cassie.

As Cassie gathered her things she smiled remembering the way her father had shaken Logan's hand and invited him back again. There had been mutual respect in the look that passed between them.

After hugs and kisses all around, Bob and Jenna herded Evan away as Logan and Cassie walked down the street to where they had left Logan's car.

When they were once again on the freeway headed back to Boston, Logan commented. "Your family doesn't live far from the city and yet Jasonville has a real small town feel to it."

"It was a great place to grow up most of the time. But I'm afraid I didn't get away with much. Of course I see things from a different perspective now and I'm thankful that there were people who cared enough to let my parents know if I was doing something dangerous."

"From the stories I heard today, I'd be willing to say that must have been all the time." Logan teased.

"I should have known better than to turn you loose with Bob," Cassie smiled." He tends to forget that he and Jenna were in on most of the stunts themselves, and those ideas weren't *all* mine."

"I'm sure you had quite a cheering section following you. I know I would have been." He grinned as he remembered her reaction upon seeing the tarantula. "Come to think of it, you climbed your desk quickly enough." He couldn't help teasing.

"Hey, you were pretty light on your feet yourself," she countered.

"You've got me there. Spiders and I haven't gotten along since I was a boy at camp."

"We were having our 'sleep out under the star's' adventure. I made the mistake of falling asleep first. Some of the guys thought it would be a good joke to pull my sleeping bag under the web of a huge garden spider. When I awoke the next morning eye to eye with the biggest spider I'd ever seen, I panicked. I screamed and started thrashing around. There were webs all over me and the worst part was that I never did find out what happened to the spider." He gave an exaggerated shiver. "I traded sleeping bags with another boy so I wouldn't have to wonder if it was still there."

Cassie was trying to hold her laughter in, but when he turned his dimples on her in a sympathetic grin, she lost her control and he joined her.

"I'm s-sorry, b-but I just can't picture you…" She gasped.

"I was glad I only had two days left at camp," He continued when they had calmed down. "I thought I'd finally controlled my fear, but when you screamed and jumped I just couldn't help myself."

"I sometimes have that effect on people."

He looked sharply at her. She had felt unattractive for so long that he wanted to be sure that she was not putting herself down. When he saw that she was smiling, he relaxed. They rode in companionable silence the rest of the way to her apartment.

Taking her key he unlocked the door for her and carried in the clothing she had changed out of earlier.

"Would you like some coffee?" she offered.

"I'd better not stay, I'm sure you have some things to do before tomorrow. I didn't give you this before because Jenna specifically said, no gifts." Reaching into his pants pocket he pulled out a small package and handed it to her. "But when I saw this I couldn't resist."

"Logan, you shouldn't have," she protested as she removed the paper. She gasped as she opened the small velvet box, which held a lovely gold cross necklace with a diamond in the center and matching earrings. "Oh Logan, it's too much," she cried, holding it out to him.

"No, It's not enough." He took her in his arms and looked deep into her eyes searching for a sign of her feelings for him.

Cupping her cheek in his palm he ran his thumb over her lips. "I haven't told you yet how very much I like your new clothes."

"Not one word." She caught her breath at the look in his eyes. Her heart began to race as she continued breathlessly. "I was beginning to wonder if you'd even noticed." She tried to concentrate as his hand slid around into her hair becoming increasingly distracting.

But it was his mouth, which closed over hers, that robbed her of all conscious thought, turning her normally obedient body to flame. She was shaken by a desire, the depth of which, she had never before experienced and she stood clinging to him in confusion. The intensity of her emotions frightened her. She was unsure if she wanted to run or throw caution to the winds and see where this new madness would take her.

Slowly he released her lips, fighting the desire that threatened to overtake them.

He hadn't meant to kiss her like that, but somehow he couldn't stop himself

He eased back and looking into her eyes saw the confusion and fear struggling with the raw emotions that were so evident. For a long moment they stood. Her head cradled in the crook of his shoulder, their breathing ragged.

"I noticed," he said huskily. Then he kissed her forehead and he forced himself to release her and walk out the door.

Chapter 7

Cassie stood on shaking legs as she stared at the door in confusion. Then forcing herself to move she stumbled forward, willing her fumbling fingers to turn the lock. She stood trembling as she leaned against the door trying to make sense of what had just happened.

Taking a deep steadying breath she made her way to the couch. Needing to hear his voice again she stared at the telephone willing it to ring, but it sat stubbornly silent.

Dropping her head into her hands she moaned as she realized how she had reacted to Logan's kiss. What must he think of her? Did he think she acted like this with every man who kissed her? Never in her life had she known that she could feel this way. Hot and cold at the same time the memory flooded over her again.

Instinctively she knew that what she felt was normal, but she was a firm believer in the sanctity of marriage. She was not naïve enough to ignore what might have happened if Logan hadn't left. What shocked her was that she hadn't wanted him to go. She was thankful that he at least had enough strength to walk away.

Her face flamed as she remembered Logan's talk of how they could get to know each other on the telephone without distractions. He had called her a distraction and he had said he was having a hard time keeping his hands off her, yet here she was showing no restraint whatsoever.

Suddenly she saw it all with startling clarity. Logan was having the same feelings that she was! She knew he liked her and had felt that he was attracted to her, but this was something different. This went far deeper and it had been growing since that first day they had made eye contact so long ago. Somehow she had failed to realize that she was deeply in love with Logan.

Love. Her hands flew to her burning cheeks, shaken to the very core of her being. She was in love with Logan. Now she understood so many things. The electricity that had seemed to flow through her whenever he was near, and the almost physic connection they seemed to have at times. This was love. Not the cozy contented feeling with a few warm kisses that she'd heard about. This was something real and... *alive!* The word came unbidden to her brain. This was what she had felt between her and Logan at the party before Jenna had hugged her and brought her down to earth.

Logan couldn't be in love with her. She mustn't let this go any farther. He hadn't reacted badly to the scars on her arm, but then he hadn't seen the rest of her. The memory of how he'd kissed the scar on her face brought a crimson glow to her skin. How would...? No she wouldn't allow her thoughts to go there. Instead she bowed her head and sought the strength and comfort she needed from the only one she knew could help her.

"Oh Lord, I don't know anything about being in love. I'm frightened because I don't know how to handle the way I feel. Help me to act according to my faith in you. I don't want to do anything that would disappoint you. And please, if it be your will, help Logan to have that same conviction, for I love him Lord, heart and soul."

The morning sun cast it's golden rays across her smiling face as in her dreams Logan prayed with her for guidance.

* * *

Logan wasn't doing quite so well. He sat in his car gripping the steering wheel in the parking garage of his apartment building. It had taken awhile for him to sort through what had happened at Cassie's apartment. His heart was sick within him as he remembered the fear he had seen in her eyes. Groaning he rested his forehead on his white knuckled hands. The last thing he had wanted was to frighten her. He had worked hard to keep his passion under control and tonight he had come close to stepping over the line.

He should have given Cassie her gift this morning, but he knew how observant her sister was and he hadn't wanted to cause her any undue embarrassment. Then when he had seen her with one lovely shoulder bared, he had wanted to put the necklace around her throat and seal it there with a kiss.

The faint scent of her perfume still clung to the front of his shirt where she had rested her head, torturing his senses. Part of him wanted to breathe it in and the other part wanted to wash himself clean of the guilt he felt at not keeping a tight enough rein on his emotions.

Walking to the elevator he wondered if he should turn around and go back and beg her forgiveness. Then he remembered the fear in her eyes. How would he be able to face her tomorrow? He was glad there had been no one in the elevator or hall as he pushed open the door of his apartment. The spacious rooms seemed devoid of life, while her tiny apartment was full of warmth and love.

He wanted to reach for the telephone, longing with all his heart to hear her voice, but what could he possibly say to her that would make her understand his love for her. He had already frightened her with the intensity of his desire and he didn't want to make matters worse.

Falling to his knees he cried out in anguish. "Father, forgive me for putting Cassie into such a volatile situation. If there is any chance I can make this right please help me to do so. I'm afraid that through my weakness I may have lost her. The fear I saw in her eyes was real and you know I don't want to hurt or frighten her. She's already been through so much. Lead me in my choice of words when I see her tomorrow and please Lord, don't let me hurt her any further. Please, show me what to do."

Logan prayed until the first rays of the sun illuminated his window. Then he rose and stood with the light of the Son shining from his face.

* * *

Cassie slipped quietly into her office and opened the appointment book. The earliest she could get Dr. Jackson in would be next week. She made a note of the date and time and was just reaching out for the telephone when she heard voices. The door to Logan's office opened and Dr. Jackson walked toward her with his hands outstretched, followed by Logan and his father Theodore Blake

"Here she is. Theo I want you to meet Cassandra Hanson the young lady we've been talking about all morning."

"We've already met, but as always, it's a pleasure to see you Cassie. There was a twinkle in Theo Blake's eyes that had Cassie wondering exactly what they had been discussing.

"Thankyou Mr. Blake, that's very kind of you." Cassie smiled politely.

"Ted here has been telling me about your accident and the treatments you have already received. He has also indicated that you might be persuaded to help us in our research." As Mr. Blake spoke Cassie couldn't help but glance toward Logan who stood slightly apart looking over some papers he was holding.

"We didn't get the chance to thoroughly discuss our proposal yesterday." Dr. Jackson was still grinning as he watched her. "I'd like to set up a meeting at my office so we can explain the procedure and draw up a schedule of treatments. We should get started right away."

"I'm afraid that's out of the question Doctor. Because of the time needed to heal I wasn't planning to start treatments until Mr. Blake leaves for England in six months on his yearly visit to the London Office.

"Something has come up and I'll be leaving tomorrow.' Logan stated. "There is a situation that needs my immediate attention in our Paris office. I need you to schedule a flight and make arrangements for a car to meet me at the airport."

"Will you be traveling alone?"

"Yes," Logan replied. He avoided her eyes as stunned by the news; Cassie automatically picked up a pen and took down the information.

Logan shook hands with the doctor and his father, biding them goodbye as he walked them to the elevator.

"I hope you know what you're doing," Theo Blake spoke in a low voice as he placed his hand on the younger man's shoulder.

"So do I." Pain showed briefly in Logan's eyes as he exchanged looks with his father.

"I'll take good care of her Son."

"I know." The elevator closed and Logan sent a quick prayer heavenward as he returned to the office.

"Here is the confirmation number for your flight." Cassie handed him the information, struggling to remain professional and not think about how very much she would miss him. "How far in advance do you want me to cancel the appointment book?"

"I'm not sure how long I'll be gone. Cancel for the next two weeks and we'll see how it goes from there. Dad explained the amount of testing Dr. Jackson has already done. Go ahead and start your treatments if you like. Have someone from the switchboard take care of the phone. If something comes up they can't handle, they can always call you. And if you need help you can feel free to call Dad." He hesitated a moment before his face softened and he gave her a wistful smile. "We can talk over lunch, but right now there's a lot of work to be done."

Nodding, she asked. "Have you notified the board members?"

"Not yet. Dad and the Doctor were waiting when I got here and I haven't had a chance to start anything yet."

Getting down to business they soon had everything under control. When lunchtime came he had her call in an order from his favorite Chinese restaurant.

They tried to eat, but neither was hungry. Pushing aside their unfinished food Cassie rose to clean up.

Reaching out Logan grasped her wrist and rubbed his hand along her forearm causing her skin to tingle. Keeping a gentle hold on her he stood and looked into her eyes. There was no fear today to cloud their emerald depths as she stood looking up at him, only pain and confusion.

"Cassie, I-" clearing his throat of the huskiness that threatened he tried again. "I'm going to miss you." Raising her hand to his lips he kissed her fingers tenderly.

Blinking back the tears that threatened her hard won composure, she drew a deep breath. "I'll miss you too," she whispered.

Carefully Logan gathered her into his arms. "I knew this would be hard, but I had no idea it would be like this." His heart beat painfully in his chest and holding her to him Logan began to pray. The words came slowly at first then with more confidence as Cassie joined him.

They had just said, 'Amen.' when the shrill sound of the telephone broke the stillness. Cassie answered, then handed the instrument to Logan. After cleaning their lunch debris she stepped into her washroom.

Examining her face in the mirror she sighed as she thought back over the last week and a half. Ten days had passed since Evan's tarantula had crawled into her office and changed everything. Such a short space of time and yet she had lived a lifetime of emotions and experiences. She was no longer, in her own eyes, just a freakish mass of hidden scars. Logan had shown her what it was like to love, and be loved for the person she is and not for the one she had been. She was slowly acknowledging that the scars, which marred her skin, did not make her ugly.

She didn't know how she would get through the next two weeks, but she knew where her strength would come from.

"Oh Father," she prayed. "I need your strength and wisdom to get through the rest of this day. Help me to be a reflection of you, I want to do your will."

When she raised her head there was a quiet peace about her. Straightening her shoulders, she walked into her office to complete preparations for Logan's departure.

The next morning the office felt different as Cassie walked in. It felt- empty. As always, when Logan had to leave on business, she felt as if something vital were missing. This time, the emptiness was more acute.

Memories of their goodbye last night were bittersweet. Even though he had held her and kissed her tenderly, she felt that he had been holding back and she couldn't help wondering if this trip was really necessary.

When she'd called the Paris office yesterday she'd had the impression that the situation Logan was going to tend to wasn't as desperate as he had made it sound.

Walking through to Logan's office she paused, her eyes on the door to his private suite. Hesitantly she knocked before turning the knob. Hoping against hope that she would find him there, but her inner radar told her even before she checked that he was gone and no matter how hard she wished for it to be so, she wouldn't find him there.

Returning to her office, she placed a call to Dr. Jackson's office. She got through to him right away.

"Cassandra?"

"When do you want to begin the treatments?"

"As soon as possible," he sounded surprised.

"That's fine with me. I'll be finished here this morning and after that I'm relatively free for the next two weeks. I only ask that you treat as large an area as you can at one time. I want to get this over with as soon as possible."

Dr. Jackson paused a moment, Cassie's voice sounded as if she were under severe strain. He wondered if she was missing Logan. They had seemed very close at the party and he was surprised that he would take an extended business trip at this time. He worried that she was pushing herself too hard and wondered if there was anything he could do.

"Doctor?"

"Yes, I was checking my schedule. Can you come in tonight at five o'clock for a consultation?"

"I'll be there, The sooner we start the sooner it will be over."

"We can start right away if you like."

"Thankyou, I'll see you tonight."

At five o'clock that evening, Theo Blake stepped into Dr. Jackson's waiting room and smiled as he approached his son's personal assistant.

"Hello Cassie, I was happy to hear that you are willing to help us."

"Hello, Mr. Blake, It's good to see you again."

"Come on back. I'll start up the equipment and when the doctor is ready we'll get down to business."

As he led the way to the back of the office Theo put his head into the doctor's study.

"Ted, I'm showing Cassie back to the therapy room. Are you coming?"

"I'll be right there. Serena should be here any minute now. I told her to come on back."

Following Theo back to the therapy room Cassie waved a greeting to Martha, Dr. Jackson's office nurse.

The room they entered was similar to the examining rooms she was accustomed to, save for a large complicated piece of equipment with tubes and wires snaking around it. There was a large treatment table in the center of the room and several stools and chairs scattered around. Theo was busy turning dials and flipping switches causing the machine to hum.

Cassie had just found a seat, in what she hoped was an out of the way corner, when Dr. Jackson entered with a woman who, though her profile was all Cassie could see, was strikingly beautiful.

Thick, glossy dark hair, an olive complexion, and perfect features devoid of make-up gave her an exotic look. She was almost as tall as Dr. Jackson, which would probably make her a few inches taller than Cassie was. Her stature, as well as her well-cut clothing, gave her an elegant quality. The way she smiled at Theo Blake made Cassie wonder if she realized that she was in love with him, and judging from the glow in Theo's eyes she could see that the feeling was mutual.

"Serena, thank you for coming. I'd like you to meet Cassie. She has also agreed to work with us." As Theo made the introductions Serena turned and Cassie caught her breath. An angry red scar spread across her left cheek and partway down her neck, marring Serena's beauty.

Cassie, who was caught off guard, smiled and tried not to react with the same shock that had hurt her so badly in the past. She was used to other people's reaction when they saw her and from her time spent at the clinic, she had some experience meeting others with similar disfigurements.

Serena's smile was warm as her eyes took in the slight scar still visible across Cassie's face. "It's wonderful to meet you Cassie, Dr. Jackson has told me that you've had a very bad experience at a young age. I'm thankful to God that I've only had my scarring for a year and a half." The woman's eye's sparkled with mischief as she turned them on Theo. "I can't say that I'm too sorry to have had it happen though. I've met some wonderful people because of it."

Theo Blake's face turned a deep crimson behind his shy grin. Cassie smiled at the confirmation that their feelings were mutual.

"Cassandra's injuries were much more extensive than yours Serena. At one time her facial scar was much worse. I'm hoping to all but eradicate it, but that's the least of our worries. There are other areas needing our immediate attention." Dr. Jackson smiled. "I'll let Theo explain how this machine works. I get too technical with my explanations, I'm afraid."

"This machine, the M-1, basically takes conventional methods one step further." Theo warmed to his subject.

"Normally lasers work on a very small area, but the M-1 can work on an area up to three times larger concentrating in the center and actually stimulating new skin growth."

"Have you ever tried it on anyone else?" Cassie asked curiously.

"Yes," Theo showed them a photograph of himself "I had a large scar on my forearm, a burn from an industrial accident many years ago. Now see for yourself." He held his arm out. There was a very faint pink area on his forearm where the scar had been.

"That's incredible." Cassie's eyes shone. "Oh Serena, I hope it works like that for you."

"And for you too." Serena smiled.

Theo explained the procedure showing the women the instrument and safety features.

"I want to warn you that even though laser treatment is often painless, because of the depth of scarring there will, undoubtedly, be considerable discomfort afterwards."

Both women understood and signed releases agreeing to the treatment.

"Now if you're ready we'll get started." Dr. Jackson smiled and handed the women each a gown asking them to change as he and Theo left the room.

Chuckling, Serena grinned at Cassie.

"The good Doctor doesn't stand much on ceremony does he. I hope you don't mind if I change with you." Serena put Cassie instantly at ease and they changed quickly.

"At least they gave us cloth gowns." Cassie smiled "I don't really care for the paper ones. They scratch and when I was still healing they were very irritating." Cassie smiled at the memory. It seemed such a long time ago.

"My biggest problem was trying to keep my clothes from rubbing these scars." Serena indicated a still painful looking scar on the side of her left breast and a corresponding one on her upper arm. "I had to walk with my hand on my hip to keep them from irritating. And forget about wearing a bra." She grinned.

Cassie, warming to the way Serena put her at ease confided. "Just wearing clothes was almost intolerable. And *itch!* I had to be constantly careful not to scratch or I'd break open. high school was not a comfortable place to be with these." While she spoke Cassie turned around and untied the top of her gown, letting it fall forward, exposing her shoulders. Serena gasped as she hurried across the room. With gentle hands she helped Cassie draw the gown up over her shoulders. Then, as she faced the younger woman, she put her arms around her in a fiercely protective hug.

"Oh, my dear how you must have suffered. I can only imagine what it must have been like for you. People can be terribly cruel and you were so young. How were you able to survive?"

"Only through prayer. And even then I'm afraid I still harbored a lot of bitterness."

"And now?" Serena scanned her face. "I see no bitterness in your eyes."

"Until recently I thought I was still freakish. And then-" She broke off blushing.

"You met the only man in the world who could make you feel beautiful again." Serena's cheeks took on a rosy hue and her eyes glowed. "I know what you mean." They stifled their laughter as a knock sounded at the door.

"Are you ready?" Dr. Jackson came in the door, followed by Theo and Nurse Martha. "Let's get started."

Pulling out a tape recorder he began to speak into it. "Test subject Cassandra is twenty-seven years old and has scarring in various degrees from an accident at age seventeen. The clean cut scars she received when she ran through a plate glass door are on her face left breast, left wrist and right thigh. She has had numerous surgeries and some conventional laser treatments. All have been documented by myself and are in her file."

"The most difficult areas to treat will be her back, shoulders, the back of the left arm and the backs of both thighs. She fell into a pile of broken glass which was ground into the skin causing numerous cuts and abrasions."

"There are also many acne like pockmarks due to splinters of glass that had festered and worked themselves out causing assorted eruptions."

As he spoke Cassie remembered the confused moment of disbelief before the intense pain had set in. For a moment she once again saw the horrified faces gathered around her as family and friends rushed to check the flow of blood, which was clouding her vision.

Serena, who noticed the pallor in Cassie's cheeks, placed an arm around her shoulders. "Are you alright?" she asked.

"I'm sorry, I'd forgotten how bad it really was. I usually try not to think about it."

"How awful for you." Serena's dark eyes were filled with anguish that she had gone through so much pain. "I'm so sorry."

"I'm okay now." Cassie flashed a reassuring smile. "Please continue Doctor."

Reassured, Dr. Jackson continued. "Test subject Serena is forty-five years old and has burn scars on the left side of her face and neck, the inside of her upper left arm and left breast due to a caustic chemical explosion. We will commence treatment on all sites."

"If you don't mind, ladies," The doctor addressed them as he picked up an instant camera. "I'd like to get some 'before pictures'. Serena?"

Serena turned her face so the doctor could get a good shot of her cheek and neck.

Theo stepped out of the room for a moment and closed the door to give them some privacy as the rest of the photos were taken.

When they had finished, Dr. Jackson called Theo in and they started the treatments.

Serena volunteered to go first and was soon finished, but Cassie, who had a lot of intricate work, took longer. Serena stayed and talked to Cassie in an effort to keep her mind occupied during her long treatment.

After dressing and receiving specialized instructions Cassie said good-bye to the doctor and walked to the door with Serena.

"Cassie, we must have lunch soon I would like to keep in touch with you outside the clinic."

"I'd like that. Let's see how things go this week before making plans. I'm not sure I'll be able to sit for awhile." She grinned ruefully giving Serena her phone number.

As she was opening the door to leave, Theo called for Cassie to wait for a moment.

"Cassie I'll be using Logan's office during the mornings all this week and I'd appreciate it if you would be available to work with me. I spoke with Logan about it before he left and we understand you will be limited by the treatment you just received. He has placed his suite at your disposal for as long as you need it."

"Thank you Mr. Blake. I'd be happy to do anything I can to help."

"Thank *you* Cassie and call me Theo. Mr. Blake and Miss. Hanson are too formal outside the office." Theo grinned.

"Certainly Mr.- Theo. I'll see you tomorrow morning. Good-bye again Serena."

As Cassie walked to her car she shook her head. Things had changed so rapidly that she hardly knew what to think.

Chapter 8

Cassie arrived at work armed with her most comfortable shoes and the least abrasive of her work suits. Driving had been difficult, as the entire left side of her body was starting to blister and she was afraid it would only get worse as her clothing continued to rub against sensitive areas. Dr. Jackson had said that the next three days would be the worst. After that the discomfort would ease up and she would have to be careful not to scratch as her body generated new skin growth.

"Good morning Cassie." Theo greeted her as he arrived. "How are you feeling today?"

"As well as can be expected," Cassie grinned. "I hope Serena is doing well."

"She probably isn't having as much trouble as you are," he eyed her as she stood gingerly. "I'm sorry, I shouldn't have asked you to come so soon after your treatment."

"It's no problem Mr. Blake. I'd just as soon be here as at home." She smiled reassuringly.

"Well, just don't hesitate to go and lie down if you need to," concern deepened the color of his eyes that were so like his son's. "And there's no reason to stand on ceremony. Please call me Theo."

"Thank you Theo. Now what can I do to help you?"

Theo had worked with Cassie before and they had gotten on well together. Today was no different. As the morning wore on he noticed more and more the cautious way she moved. Finally he asked her if she had taken any of the pain medication Dr. Jackson had prescribed for her.

"No, I didn't want to be sleepy or dull my thinking." Seeing his concern she rushed to continue. "It's okay, I hardly ever take the painkillers the doctor prescribes for me."

"But why?"

"I don't like the way the pills make me feel." Cassie blushed. "I'd rather put up with a little discomfort than have to go through that again."

"Don't you take anything to help with the pain?"

"Over the counter medications."

"And when was the last time you took them?" He eyed her suspiciously.

"When I left my apartment." Cassie looked at her watch surprised that so much time had elapsed.

Theo picked up the telephone and spoke to the cafeteria. Asking them to send up two orders of whatever they were serving that day.

In a tone that brooked no argument, he told her to take her medication and go lie down until their food got there.

Cassie didn't argue, it felt good to stretch out on her side on Logan's bed. The left side of her body was sore and she was tired from standing and trying to sit in a way that kept the pressure off her left leg and back.

She blushed as she remembered the last time she lay here. Trying to keep her mind free of 'distractions' she forced herself to relax. Closing her eyes she caught the scent of Logan's cologne on the pillow and immediately was enveloped in a cocoon of well being as she prayed silently for him.

Theo knocked quietly on the bedroom door and called to let her know their lunch was there, but he got no response from her. When he opened the door to check on her he found her sound asleep. Moving quietly, he carefully drew a sheet over her and left her to rest. With no painkillers he wondered if she had slept at all last night.

Shaking his head he went back to work. Cassie was a special woman. He was again amazed by her efficiency in the office as well as her determination to be of service. She'd been working with Logan for so long that he felt she must know as much about the company as his son did. There was no doubt that she was an incredible asset, not only to the company, but also as a potential daughter-in-law.

He smiled as he remembered the story Ted Jackson told him about the way Logan had reacted at Cassie's birthday party. Yes, he smiled, she was definitely daughter-in-law potential and it was about time.

* * *

"Cassie?" Someone was calling her name.

She didn't want to wake up, she'd been dreaming that she was held safe in Logan's arms.

"Cassie?" There it was again, Slowly she opened her eyes still wrapped in the warmth of her dream. A smile played over her features as she saw his eyes. Piercing blue and fraught with concern.

"Logan?" she murmured sleepily reaching for him. Then her vision cleared and she saw Theo's face.

Abruptly she pulled her hand back, stifling a gasp.

"Cassie, it's four-thirty and I was heading home, but I didn't want to leave without telling you." Theo smiled kindly.

She winced as she struggled to sit up.

"I'm sorry I had no idea..."

"It's perfectly alright. You had a rough night and needed the sleep I just wanted you to know I was leaving." He ran an assessing eye over her." I can either get someone else to help me or you can bring a few things and stay here if you like."

"I'll be fine," she gingerly got off the bed. "I'm sorry, I'm afraid I was worthless to you this afternoon."

"On the contrary, you have been a great help. Not only as an assistant, but also as a patient." Concern showed in his face as he continued. "I think we treated too large an area at once and believe me, I'll let the good doctor know about it.

"No, Dr. Jackson didn't want to treat such a large area, but I asked him to. I didn't realize you would need me to work and I wanted to get it over with as soon as possible."

"Before Logan returns?"

She nodded as she ran her hands over her clothes and hair making sure everything was tidy.

"Yes, I wanted to get it out of the way, so when he came back, I'd be ready to return to work." There was a wistful light in her eyes as she straightened the bed.

"Cassie?" Theo spoke hesitantly.

"Yes?"

"I think there are some things you need to know. Come have a seat." Theo led the way into the sitting room. "Or you can stand if you wish." He smiled as she gingerly perched on the arm of the chair.

"This is fine," she grinned. "Thanks for your consideration."

Theo paced the length of the room. Returning he stopped in front of her with a serious look.

"I'm not sure how to begin," he sighed. "Joanna, Logan's mother was more than just my wife, she was my partner. When she died I'm afraid a large part of me went with her, including the desire to keep Blake International running." He closed his eyes as a paroxysm of pain swept over his face. "I couldn't eat, I couldn't sleep. Every time I closed my eyes I saw the shock on her face as the machine blew up."

Cassie's expressive eyes filled with tears, as she understood what he was telling her. "You were working on the apparatus at the time of the explosion. Oh Theo I'm so sorry. Now I understand why you were so devastated."

"It took quite awhile to come to terms with my loss. I know this sounds strange but for a long time I was afraid to live. Fearing that my going on with my life would, in some way, mar the love I'd had with my Annie." Shaking his head he continued.

"I failed to realize what I was doing to my son. I am not sure, but I think Logan is afraid."

"Afraid of what?" Cassie asked puzzled.

"Of himself, of loving too deeply. My own guilt nearly destroyed me and I'm afraid it may have had a lasting effect on Logan." He now knew what he had to ask her. "I'm sorry to be so personal, but what exactly is your relationship with Logan?"

Cassie blushed crimson. "What do you mean?"

"I know you are in love with him. I saw it in your eyes when you awoke," he looked amused. "Don't be embarrassed, I'm very happy you feel this way. I can't think of anyone more perfect for Logan. He has thought of nothing but work for far too long. It's high time he started thinking about his future."

"Forgive me for being indelicate. I'm just trying to figure out why my son, who is always so much in control of himself, should run off to Paris when it wasn't really necessary." He watched the play of emotion as he confirmed her thoughts that Logan had left when he didn't really need to.

"I don't know exactly why he left. I was as surprised as you are. I thought things were fine between us and then, well, he's gone." There was a lost look about her that made Theo want to comfort her.

"I'm sorry, I shouldn't have asked such a personal question. It was unforgivable of me."

"No, you have a right to ask. You want what is best for the company and Logan shouldn't have left you in the lurch like this." A plan began to take form in her mind. If Theo could play matchmaker then so could she.

"Why not? I left him 'in the lurch' when I lost Annie."

"But that was different, your wife had just died and no one could blame you for falling apart like you did." Cassie's look was sympathetic. "How long has it been?"

"Eleven years, sometimes it seems like yesterday."

"And sometimes like a lifetime ago. That's how I feel about my accident. You know," she cast him a thoughtful glance. "One of the things Logan has helped me to see is that when I put my life on hold I didn't cease to live. I only ceased to enjoy life. Does that make sense to you?"

"Perfect sense. Why do we do this to ourselves?" He asked with a smile.

"I know I did it out of fear. I was afraid to look into someone's eyes and see the truth staring me in the face. Physically, I was no longer the person I thought I was. I couldn't look in the mirror and reconcile the person I saw there with the one I knew myself to be." She shook her head and smiled.

"It's strange to be disembodied like that." Theo shook his head.

"I guess that's one of the reasons I'm willing to get these treatments. Apart from the pulling and discomfort, I want to close that chapter on my life. I'm ready to move forward, and the only way to do that is to ease the scars, stop hiding and accept them as a part of my life. A part that will never completely go away."

"I know that you can't erase all the damage and I'm actually rather happy you can't. I think it will do me good to have a reminder sometimes. Then, if I ever feel tempted to stop living again, I'll remember how it feels to watch everyone else go on with their lives while I sat in a vacuum."

"Logan taught you all that?" Theo smiled as Cassie blushed again.

"Well, he doesn't know how different I look when I see myself through his eyes."

"I can see how big an impact he's had on you and by the way he ran off, I believe you've had the same effect on him."

"Why do you say that?"

"Well, to start with, Logan's never backed away from something he wanted in his life. It stands to reason that he doesn't want to push you until you are ready." He grinned. "He just doesn't know that you're ready."

"He's a lot like his father." Cassie laughed.

"What?"

"I said, he's a lot like you." Her eyes twinkled. "While we are analyzing ourselves, perhaps we should bring up Serena."

"What has she got to do with this?" Now it was Theo's turn to blush.

"I saw the way you looked at each other. I know it's none of my business, but I think she would make Logan a wonderful stepmother. Maybe then he would quit worrying about you so much."

"Serena is a lovely woman, but she's ten years younger than I am. I think she would do better with someone who doesn't come with so much emotional baggage."

"I don't think there is someone like that Theo." Cassie said thoughtfully. "Everyone has his or her own 'baggage'. God forgives us and helps us to make good choices, but when we make a mess out of our lives, He doesn't instantly take all the trouble away. *We* have to learn how to deal with the mess we've made."

"'You reap what you sow.'"

"Yes." She watched him gauging the impact of her next words "Perhaps the reason Serena agreed to the treatments was because she no longer feels that she could catch the attention of a man like you."

He made a frustrated gesture and began pacing again. "That's ridiculous! Why Serena is not only beautiful, but she's intelligent, thoughtful and..." He stopped, staring into space and sighed heavily. "And just about as close to perfect as she can get."

"Then why are you here watching over me when you can be there watching over her?"

"I promised Lo-" he broke off shame faced.

"What?" Cassie smiled slightly bemused. "Logan asked you to watch over me?"

"I told him I'd take care of you while he's gone. He was worried about you."

"I see." Her frustration was showing. "He was so worried that he went tearing off half way around the world. You say he's afraid. Well, he doesn't have to be afraid of me."

"Now wait a minute. When I said he was afraid, I meant, afraid of himself. As far as I can make out, things must have heated up a little between you. Am I right?"

Cassie sputtered ineffectively, while her face gave her away.

"I'm sorry, I don't mean to pry," Theo grinned unrepentantly. "But, you see, Logan taught a Sunday school class of teenaged boys and he was constantly counseling them not to get into a situation where things might get out of control. He's a real stickler for not carrying things too far before marriage. I believe that this is just the sort of thing that he would do if he felt he couldn't control himself."

"So this is what you've been trying to get at all this time? You think Logan is afraid that he can't physically control himself?" She asked incredulous. "It's clear that you don't know your son very well." Cassie thought that Logan had exercised admirable control. "Look I don't think this is getting us anywhere."

"I agree with you there. I think you should call him and see for yourself why he went. Or better yet go to Paris."

"What?"

"Go to Paris."

"I can't do that. For one thing I can't even sit in the seat long enough to get out of the airport."

He grinned. "Then use the next best thing." He pointed to the telephone. "I'll make you a deal, you use the company phone and call Logan. He should be at his hotel. He's still awake, I spoke with him before I woke you. And I'll call Serena."

"Now I see who taught your son how to maneuver a board member into a corner," Cassie grinned and looked at her watch. "Okay, *I'll* call Logan, but *you* have to go and *see* Serena."

"And I see he taught *You* the fine art of negotiation," he reached out his hand. "It's a deal." They solemnly shook hands on it.

Chapter 9

Paris may be one of the most romantic cities in the world, but to Logan it was hot and overcrowded. He had been walking all evening, trying to dispel the feeling of loneliness that threatened to overtake him at every turn. Everywhere he looked there were things he wanted to share with Cassie.

Familiar sights no longer held an appeal for him. He had prayed almost continually as he walked, worry for Cassie uppermost in his prayers.

When his father had called his cell phone earlier that evening, he said that she was asleep in his suite. He had praised her work, as well as her character, saying that she wouldn't complain even though he could see that she was in pain.

The knowledge of her discomfort was almost more than he could bear and his heart cried out to his Heavenly Father to relieve her suffering. He felt powerless to protect her from the pain he knew she both feared and welcomed.

Checking his watch, he wondered if she were awake yet. What was his father thinking having her work when she needed to be resting?

Finally he resolved to call her and find out for himself how she was doing. He returned to the hotel and as he opened the door the telephone started ringing. Wanting to call Cassie he impatiently picked up the receiver and barked, "Yes?"

"Logan?"

"Cassie, is that you?" His heart beat heavily as he fell into a nearby chair.

"Yes, have I caught you at a bad time?"

"No, I just got in. Is everything okay?"

"Yes, I uh- was talking to your father and well..." Embarrassed, she stumbled to a halt, she had never precipitated a personal telephone conversation to a man in her life.

"Did Dad tell you I called?" A slow smile spread over his face.

"Yes," she hesitated not knowing how to tell him how desperately she missed him. "I just-"

"I'm glad you called," he broke in. "I've missed you."

Her heart took wings. "I've missed you too."

"Dad said you're having a lot of pain."

"You're father worries too much. I'm just fine."

"Cassie, You don't have to do this." His voice was heavy with concern. "You are already beautiful."

She paused a moment all the old feelings of inadequacy coming to the fore. She knew that he must be made to understand how important it was for her to get the treatments she had been waiting for. But how?

"I know that the treatments are optional at this point and I don't want to argue with you, but I know what you can't see," she sighed. "Logan there's a lot more to my scarring than just my face and arm."

"What happened?"

"I ran through a plate glass door," she said impatiently.

"No, I mean after that. Something happened to make you feel like this. Someone hurt you." The knuckles of the hand holding the receiver turned white as he asked with deadly calm. "Who called you ugly?"

"It doesn't matter, it was a long time ago." Cassie tried to pass him off.

"It does matter. Someone hurt you." He forced himself to remain calm. He knew, if she would open up to him he might finally get to the bottom of what had happened so long ago. His voice grew soft and persuasive, turning her resolve into mush. "Please Cassie, tell me about it?"

The bitter taste of panic welled up within her. How could she possibly tell him of that long ago day when her heart had been turned to stone and shattered by what she had heard?

'*Tell him.*' The thought came unbidden to her heart. Gripping the phone, she fought the rising tide of hysteria that threatened to overtake her. Surely, God knew that she couldn't reveal the awful pain that she had kept hidden for so long.

'*Tell him.*' The words came to her again stirring up memories she had long ago buried. She realized that she had never brought the hurt out into the open and allowed God to help her work through her pain. Instead she had pushed the hurtful words deeper and deeper into her past until they, like the glass fragments, had festered, causing sickness in her spiritual body.

Her heart cried out, 'Father forgive me,' and the lock she had placed on that secret place of painful memories fell open. Once the words started to flow, she could no longer hold them back.

"It was my senior year of high school. I was in the restroom trying to get my arm to quit bleeding. A fragment of glass had worked its way out and I was sick of the nurse's office. I heard someone coming and hid in the farthest stall so they wouldn't see me."

"There were several girls. I heard them talking about me." Staring into space, she once again heard the voices that she had hidden from for so long. "I knew, of course, that people talked about me, but," she sighed. "I had no idea." Her pain was evident as she thought back on that day.

"I couldn't move, I couldn't even breathe, I was so afraid they would know I was there. They said that I was a becoming a drug addict from the pain medication I was on and I was so ugly they couldn't even look at me without getting sick. I heard words associated with me that I'd only heard in a horror story that I tried to read once when I was ten-years-old."

Tears fell unchecked down her face as she continued. "Sadie tried to defend me. I could tell that she felt guilty because I was looking for her when I ran through the glass. Then they said that some of the guys were daring each other to go out with me. I was nothing but a big joke. They even said that Bob threw me over for Jenna because I was a freak. They didn't know that I was the one who broke off with him." Her voice shook with the force of her memories.

"I covered my ears so I couldn't hear anything else, but I got sick to my stomach and had to put my hands over my mouth. After they left I couldn't stop crying. I hid out until everyone had gone home for the day. I couldn't look anyone in the face after that. I was so humiliated. I wanted to hide in my room forever. Even when I healed up enough to wear make-up, I still hid. I stopped looking anyone in the eyes for fear of what I might see."

"Then, I went to college in another state, where no one knew me. I thought I could get on with my life. I even started to date a guy, but when I told him about the accident and showed him my arm he got sick." Her voice caught on a sob.

"You are the only one I ever showed my arm to that didn't come unglued and my arm is just the tip of the iceberg. My back and leg are covered with more of the same scarring and there are other scars too. I'm grateful for your strength of character and your desire to make me feel like more than I am, but I know I'm not beautiful like you say. I'm nothing but an ugly mass of scars, inside and out and now that you know the truth, you won't want me either." Her voice ground to a stop on a hoarse whisper and she waited with her heart in her throat to hear what he would say. Now that he knew what a mess she was, he would stop seeing her. He had already gone to France to get away from her.

There was silence for a moment and she was about to hang up the phone, sure that he was disgusted by her revelations. Then he spoke in a voice so fraught with emotion that she was left in no doubt that what he said was the absolute truth.

"Cassie my darling, I know you don't understand why I left. I didn't understand it all either until this moment. If I were with you right now there is no way I could keep myself from showing you just how beautiful you are." His breathing was ragged as he admitted. "I frightened you once with the intensity of my feelings for you and I won't allow myself to do it again. You've suffered too much hurt in the past and as God is my witness, I will not allow anyone to hurt you again!"

As he spoke the darkness that had surrounded that part of her life for so long burst into brightness as God gently wiped away the pain she had experienced. Now in the light of love there was no longer any reason to hold on to it. Through Logan, she saw a small portion of the unconditional love that God had for her and she was humbled.

A tremulous smile broke out across Cassie's face as she whispered. "Thank you, that means more to me than you'll ever know."

"Oh Cassie," he groaned.

Conscious of what Theo had told her, she knew that she must make certain there were no longer any misunderstandings between them.

"Logan there's something I need to tell you." Closing her eyes she breathed deeply praying for strength. "I've never been frightened of *you*. I-I have never felt like this before and the other night it was *my* reaction to you, that I was afraid of. When you kissed me that night I was completely blindsided by how I felt. What I was feeling wasn't only physical. I-it was-love." Gripping the telephone as if it was a lifeline she waited with her heart in her throat for him to speak.

"Logan?"

He released the breath he hadn't realized he was holding. "Say it again." He begged.

Light headed, she poured all her feeling into the words. "I love you, Logan."

"Thank God! Oh Cassie, I've loved you since the first moment I saw you."

"I think I must have fallen in love with you at the same time. I was just too messed up to know it." Suddenly she was light headed from the release of the strain she had been held under for so long and a bubble of laughter escaped her. "Have you ever in your life heard of two such hard-headed people?"

"Never!" He joined her laughter as the tension broke within him.

"I can't believe you love me," she sighed tenderly. "I was afraid you left because you didn't want to be around me anymore. I was ready to quit my job and move to another city if I had to."

"I wouldn't have allowed it. I'd have found you and begged you to come back."

Cassie sighed happily, "I hope Theo and Serena are doing as well as we are."

"Who?"

"Your father is hopelessly in love with a lovely woman named Serena and she feels the same toward him. He was on his way to see her when he left here." She told him what she had learned about his father.

"My father's in love. How did you manage that?"

"I didn't silly, God did it. Just like he did for us." Suddenly she shone with a joyous brightness. "Oh Logan I'm so happy. When are you coming home?"

"Not until you heal enough for me to hold you, although not being able to hold you might have its advantages," he chuckled.

"In that case I'll have the doctor get started with the next treatment right away."

Laughing and teasing they talked for another hour, then noticing the time, Cassie rang off, aware of the six-hour time difference. Logan needed to rest so he could finish his work and come home. And she needed to get home and treat the small blisters she could feel across her back and thigh.

The next evening Jenna called after she finished talking to Logan and was surprised when Cassie told her that Logan was out of the country. Then when she told her that she had started her treatments Jenna was very upset that she hadn't been called upon to help her sister. She was even more upset when she found out how extensive the treatment had been.

"Are you crazy?" Jenna cried appalled.

Cassie couldn't help laughing, "Yes, I'm totally and irrevocably crazy."

"Cassie, You're scaring me. Are you on pain medication?"

"You know me better than that. This is much, much better," Cassie couldn't stop smiling. "I'm in love!"

"Well, it's about time you finally figured it out. I've known for ages." Jenna laughed delightedly. "Have you told Logan?"

"Yes, we talked yesterday."

"I can't understand you two. Why in the world did you wait to tell him until he was in a foreign country?"

"We didn't do it this way on purpose. It just happened."

"When is the wedding?"

"Jenna! I just realized I'm in love." Cassie laughed. "Besides, he hasn't asked me and I don't know if he will."

"Well, one thing's for sure. Judging how he looked at you, I'd say, it won't be long."

"I hope not."

"Cassie I'm shocked!" Jenna giggled. "Okay, I'm not really."

"You shouldn't be. I remember *your* first real kiss."

"What?"

"Your first *real* kiss was in my hospital room. I'm sure you remember it, I do. After all I was laying right next to you."

"You were awake?" Jenna was scandalized. "Why didn't you let us know you weren't sleeping."

"What, and ruin the mood? I don't think so. I was so happy that I was afraid you would see my tears and misconstrue how I felt. I'm assuming that Bob got better at it with practice. I haven't seen him step on your toe lately."

"I don't know what to say. I was in love with Bob for so long, but all he could see was you. Then when he came up behind me and wrapped his arms around me at the party I was so mad. I wanted him to love *me*, not you. Then when you were hurt I felt so guilty for being jealous. I thought you loved him and I was miserable," she sighed. "When you told him you didn't love him I wasn't sure what to think. Then that night when he kissed me…" Embarrassed she came to a stop.

"Fireworks lit up the sky and your bones all turned to water. While the whole time you felt as if your feet weren't quite touching the floor." Cassie volunteered.

"You are in love." Jenna laughed. "I just need to know one thing."

"And what would that be?"

"Of the three wedding dresses I have on display, which one do you want."

"Isn't that jumping the gun a bit?" Cassie laughed.

"Not if you remember the 'fireworks'. I have a feeling-"

"A feeling?" Oh all right, who am I to argue with one of your 'feelings'."

They discussed dresses for awhile before Jenna rang off. Then smiling to herself Cassie went off to bed to dream of white satin and lace.

Chapter 10

Cassie met with Serena for lunch after work the next day. She was thankful that Serena had chosen The Old Country Tearoom for lunch. Instead of booths, comfortable chairs and settees were arranged with screens and potted plants to create small private sitting rooms. The cheerful chintz of the furniture and curtains lent a bright homey atmosphere you could relax in while enjoying a meal or an afternoon tea.

Serena smiled as she poured coffee from the polished silver pot into the delicate china cups the waitress had brought them after their meal. "I chose this restaurant with you in mind. I thought the settee would be more comfortable for you then a regular chair."

"It is, thank you. Now tell me why you look so happy. Does it have anything to do with Theo?" Cassie asked with a smile.

"It might, but you must tell me of your happiness also." Serena smiled. "I can tell something has happened."

"I talked with your future son-in-law last night."

Serena blushed, "Future…How did you know? Did Theo tell you?"

"No. I couldn't get anything out of him this morning, and he couldn't keep from smiling."

"I could tell the moment you walked through the door. All I had to do was look into your eyes.' Cassie grinned. "And all through the meal, you've radiated happiness. Theo is a very lucky man. Do you have a date set?"

"Not yet. He just asked me last night."

"If you're interested I could give you the number of a wonderful dress designer."

"I'd appreciate that. I don't want a big fancy wedding. Just something simple and personal."

"I know what you mean. Just close friends and family is a perfect arrangement."

"It'll be mostly just friends for me. I lost my parents five years ago. My father died of cancer and my mother died shortly thereafter, she missed him dreadfully." Serena smiled, "But, they weren't apart for long."

"Do you have any brothers or sisters?"

"No, just an aunt who never married, but what about you? Are you going to be my daughter-in-law?"

Cassie laughed, "You never can tell. I can't think of anyone I'd like more as a mother-in-law than you."

"When Logan comes home you need to do something special to entice him into asking you."

"I don't think that would be a good idea," Cassie blushed to the roots of her hair.

"I wasn't suggesting you wear a belly dancer outfit," Serena grinned. "Just something special."

"My sister Jenna, who is the designer I told you about, has made me some lovely clothes but no belly dancer outfits." Cassie laughed. Motioning to her attire she continued. "I usually only wear suits at the office."

"I'm sure she's wonderful. I just hope she's fast. Theo doesn't want to wait too long and I agree, after all, it's not like we just met. We've known each other since long before my accident."

"How long ago did that happen?"

"A year and a half ago. A caustic solution I was working with blew up. I'm so thankful that I was the only one who was injured.

The young woman I was working with was across the room at the time."

"It must have been very painful."

"It was, both physically and emotionally." A shadow crossed her features at the memory. "At first I was tempted to hide away. Then I realized that it was the perfect witnessing tool. When people asked what happened I used the opportunity to tell them how the Lord protected me." Her eyes shone as she related some of the instances in which her scar had opened up a line of communication with people she normally wouldn't have spoken with. "When God places something so profound in your lap, I believe you should use it."

"I wish I had known you when I had my accident. Maybe I wouldn't have let some of my experiences get to me so badly." Cassie explained what had happened when she overheard the girls in the restroom.

"I'm afraid I didn't react in a very Christian like way. Instead of using my injuries for God's glory, I hid. I hid behind pretended indifference, long sleeves and high necklines. Then, when I'd healed enough, I hid behind heavy make-up and a mask of professionalism. I refused to use the perfect witnessing tool the Lord gave me and instead I clung to anonymity." Shaking her head she continued.

"If no one noticed me I wouldn't have to deal with their reaction to what they saw when I looked in a mirror." She shook her head. "How could I have been so blind?"

"I don't think you were blind, just very young." Serena leaned forward. "Sometimes we have our own idea of how we want to live our lives and we haven't the slightest clue that God has a different path he wants us to walk.

"We've both been through major changes in our lives. Life changes happen every day. Some are large and some are small. It's a lot like turning the pages in a book. At times the pages are wrenched from our hands like in the case of our accidents. Other times you have the option to turn the page on past experiences. If you aren't willing to move on you will cease to grow. There have been times in my life when I felt I was definitely on the wrong page." Serena smiled sadly.

"For a while I tried to go back to a time when there was no hurt, no staring eyes, and no embarrassment over my looks. I tried to pretend that nothing had happened, but I couldn't. There was always a reminder waiting for me in the mirror. When I realized I couldn't go back, I knew there was only one way *to* go."

"Forward," Cassie smiled as she picked up where Serena left off. "Denial is one way to try to keep from the path the Lord has for us. My father, who is a minister, says that everyone has his or her own path to walk. If we walk with the Lord he shines his light for us, if not we stumble around in the darkness. I'm afraid I've done an awful lot of stumbling around."

Clasping her new friend by the hand Serena smiled. "I want you to pray for me, that I will walk the path that God has for me. And I'll pray for you too."

Cassie returned her smile. "The Bible says, *'Thy word is a lamp unto my feet and a light unto my path.'* My dad has said over and over that God gave us the Bible as a road map, but sometimes the signposts seem to be obscured and we still need to stop now and then and ask Him for directions along the way. I'd love to pray with you."

Quietly, in the privacy of their 'sitting room', the women prayed for guidance, with hands clasped and joined hearts.

After saying goodbye, Cassie walked to her car thinking about what she and Serena had talked about. She realized she had been hiding too long and it was time for a change.

On impulse she slipped into a clothing shop and stood looking around wondering if she had suddenly gone mad. A sales girl was approaching and Cassie was just turning to flee when she stopped and stared, mesmerized by the lovely creation she saw before her. It was beautiful. The scoop neckline and narrow shoulder straps promised comfort while the embossed satin fabric fell softly away in a flowing sweep to a wide hemline. The pattern was a riot of colors ranging from a rich russet to deep salmon flowers on a background of dark green palm fronds

"Isn't it gorgeous." The sales girl murmured at Cassie's side. "The shades are perfect with your dramatic coloring. Would you like to try it on?" With a sweeping glance she picked out the right size and escorted Cassie to the fitting room. "Let me know if you need any help."

'Here I go being crazy again Lord,' she thought as she carefully changed into the soft dress. The fabric swirled across the tops of her feet as she turned before the mirror. The damaged skin on her arm and back stood out in stark relief to the beauty of the garment and she sighed as she changed back into her original clothing.

Walking out of the fitting room she had every intention of leaving the dress hanging on the return rack and was surprised when instead, she handed it to the sales girl.

"I'll take it." Was that her voice she wondered as she blushed?

"I knew you would like it. I have one myself and it makes me feel so feminine to wear it. Is there something else I can show you?"

"Not now, this is quite different from the clothes I usually wear." Taking a deep breath she sent a quick prayer heavenward as she plunged on. "I was in an accident ten years ago that left me with severe scarring and since then I've haven't felt comfortable wearing something that allowed the scars to show. This is the first item in my new wardrobe."

As Cassie had hoped the girl asked about the accident and for the next half an hour, not one person interrupted them as Cassie unfolded the timeless story of salvation to a hungry soul.

That night Cassie couldn't keep the elation from her voice as she told Logan about her lunch with Serena and witnessing to the sales girl. "I can't believe I missed such an important opportunity as this. I thought it was my father's job to use this kind of illustration in his sermons. I had no idea that the Lord wanted *me* to use it."

"Your experience has been very different from Serena's." Logan was thoughtful. "I don't think the Lord expected you, at that age, to know how to handle such a situation. When we're hit by an unexpected tragedy we don't always understand how to react. We just go on instinct and later it doesn't do any good to beat ourselves up over it. The main thing is that we learn from our mistakes and do all we can not to repeat them."

The wisdom of Logan's words struck Cassie's heart. This man had so many unplumbed depths and she wanted to get to know them all.

"Serena is a special woman. I hope your father knows just how incredible she is."

"I think he has a pretty good idea of it. I asked him about Serena when I talked to him earlier. He was evasive at first, but when I told him how happy I was for him, he admitted that he had asked her to marry him." His father had had a few questions of his own, but Logan wasn't ready to reveal them to her yet.

"They've been in love for a long time, they just wouldn't admit it. I think they'll do fine." Cassie mused. "He's trying not to show it, but he's terribly preoccupied."

"He ought to try having the object of his affections in the same office. It's a wonder I ever got anything done."

Remembering the day Evan's spider had interrupted the mess she was making on her computer Cassie laughed merrily. "Oh heaven forbid. I'm afraid having Serena at the office would be a disaster."

You have a wonderful laugh." Logan smiled as he remembered the way she looked at the beach laughing joyously at him as he raced after her. A longing so strong it nearly took his breath away stole over him. He drew a deep breath and said in a husky voice, "I wish I was finished here, but it will take another week to sort through the rest of this mess."

Cassie's eyes filled with tears and she tried to clear her throat speaking in a hoarse whisper. "I can hardly wait. I've missed you terribly."

"What are you doing this weekend?" He asked trying to get back on safe footing again.

"I'll probably straighten up the apartment, then go out to Mom and Dad's. Theo is finished at the office so I'll probably stay in Jasonville next week."

"Take the cell phone from my desk drawer so I can call you while you're gone."

"Hmm, okay, but I'd rather take you"

"You could come to Paris."

"Did your Father put that idea into your head?"

"No, why?"

"He tried to get me to fly over there when we talked on Wednesday." She smiled as she remembered how they had tried to out maneuver each other.

"Why didn't you? The staff was wondering why you didn't come and your passport is updated."

"I could hardly sit down," she laughed. "It's much better already. I can't believe how quickly I'm healing this time."

"Have you ever been to Paris when you weren't on business?"

"The only overseas traveling I've done was with you. Some day I'd like to go for the fun of it."

"There are so many places you must see, Paris, Rome, Venice, London. Where would you like to go?"

"The place I would most like to visit is New Zealand. I've read a lot about it and I've seen some travel films. It sounds beautiful."

"I've been to a lot of places, but I've never been to New Zealand. What have you heard about it that makes you want to visit there?"

He enjoyed the soft tones of her voice and as he listened, asking occasional questions to keep her talking. He had discovered quite by accident while visiting with Bob that she not only had a gift for business, but she was an inveterate storyteller. He'd said that she could keep the children spellbound for hours as she spun her tales. She could definitely keep him spellbound for the rest of his life. He so looked forward to their nightly calls that he gladly cut his sleep time as short as she would let him. There would be plenty of time to sleep on the twelve-hour flight back to Boston.

Most of his plans were already in motion and he prayed that everything would go well with his meeting next weekend. He sent a quick prayer heavenward for strength and guidance. Never had he felt so nervous at the thought of an upcoming meeting.

"Logan, are you asleep?" Cassie chuckled.

"No, I was held spellbound by the sound of your voice." Logan grinned. "I'm becoming enthralled by the thought of visiting New Zealand, it sounds like a wonderful place."

"You're not even home from Paris yet and your already talking about going somewhere else?"

"I didn't say I was leaving again right away. There are far too many distractions in Boston right now for me to get away for awhile."

"Here we go with the distractions again. You simply must learn to keep your mind under control," she teased.

"I'm working on it," he murmured.

"Oh my goodness, look at the time. I need to get off of here so you can get some sleep before you have to be up again. I don't know how you can function on so little rest." She had been having a hard time sleeping herself. Most nights she lay awake praying and trying to avoid thoughts of Logan. She was aware that he was under a tremendous amount of pressure. The company was running smoothly here in the States and from what information she received working with Theo, she knew that Logan was dealing with the problems in France in record time. Intuitively, she could sense an undercurrent of stress as she spoke with him tonight.

After their nightly prayers she hung up and spent the rest of the afternoon and evening doing laundry and cleaning her apartment.

The next morning, she got up early, finished her normal weekend chores, and packed to spend the week with her family. She stopped and did a little shopping on her way to Jasonville and was soon having lunch with her parents.

After she helped clean up from lunch Cassie excused herself and changed into the new swimsuit she had just bought. Looking in the mirror she took a steadying breath as she took stock of her reflection. The light tan she had acquired had faded somewhat, but now that the blisters had healed she would be able to resume her visits to the tanning salon. The one-piece swimsuit she had bought was a rich emerald green with an exotic array of tiger lilies. It reminded her of the new dress she had bought. She shook her head at her boldness. She had planned to buy basic black, but when she had seen this she knew it was the perfect 'coming out' suit.

Wearing a white toweling robe she headed for the pool. Glancing around, she failed to see her mother standing in the shadows of the kitchen watching her through the window.

Dropping her robe on the chaise lounge she slowly made her way to the steps leading into the water. The sun beat down hot on her as she paused for a moment with her face upturned toward the light.

Rev. Hanson stepped into the kitchen and hurried over to his wife who was staring out the window with tears streaming down her face. With a finger to her lips for silence she pointed out the window. He was just in time to see his daughter slide into the water and swim across the pool.

"When did Jenna get here?" He asked not understanding the import of what he was seeing.

"That's not Jenna." Choked Melissa.

"What?" He took another look as Cassie climbed out of the pool and walked around to where she could dive. Seeing the scars he stared open mouthed.

"Praise God," he breathed. "It's our Cassie." He put his arms around his wife and they stood together watching their daughter swim for the first time in ten years.

After about fifteen minutes Cassie climbed out of the pool and carefully dried off. She had just put on her robe when her parents walked out with tall glasses of lemonade.

"Are you wearing sunscreen?" Melissa asked as she passed her daughter a glass.

"Not this time. I didn't want to irritate the new growth of skin and Dr. Jackson said it would be good to get some sun." Taking a sip she put her drink down and donned the robe.

"I approve of your choice of swimwear." Her father cleared his throat.

"Thanks Dad." Cassie mumbled as he gently hugged her before turning her over to her mother.

Wiping his eyes, Rev. Hanson stood listening to the half-formed questions and answers his wife and daughter were uttering. If he lived a million years he would never understand how they could communicate like this.

Laughing and crying they all took seats in the shade and Cassie filled them in on much of what had transpired.

"Thank God Logan had to go to Paris. I believe the Lord knew it would be wise to separate the two of you until you sort this thing out and decide where to go from here."

Just then they heard voices coming from the front and Evan and his mother entered through the gate. Jenna quickly took in the situation and a beatific smile spread across her face as she approached the group.

"The rumors are true, the mermaid is back." Jenna's eyes danced as she kissed her sister's cheek. "You aren't wearing the bikini are you?"

"No, even Dad approves of this suit." Opening her robe she shyly showed her sister her new swimsuit. As Jenna exclaimed over the colors and line of the suit, Bob who had just joined the group, spoke up with a huge smile.

"Hey there little sister," he cleared his throat. "It's nice to see you back. You've been missing for a long time."

"She was here at the party Dad." Evan broke in. "Hey no fair. How come Aunt Cassie can write on her an' Mom says I can't write on me?"

"What are you talking about Evan?" Jenna faced her son.

"Aunt Cassie wrote on her leg, see?" He pointed to the scar on Cassie's thigh. It did look like someone had written on her in red marker.

Cassie smiled at her nephew and addressed the rest of the group.

"It does look like marker. Doesn't Evan know?"

"He knows about the accident." Jenna looked puzzled. " I guess I just assumed he knew about the scars, but I guess there's really no reason he should."

Cassie held her hand out to Evan and when the little boy approached her she sat down and pointed to the line on her leg. "This isn't from a marker Evan, it's a scar. Here, feel it," she ran her finger across it.

"Remember hearing about my accident? Cassie explained briefly what happened as he fingered the scar.

"There are other scars too, see?" Taking off her robe she showed him the damage on her back and explained. "Uncle Pete wasn't going to come to the party because he had to work, but God knew what was going to happen and He fixed it so Uncle Pete got off early and was there when I needed him."

"Wow! If God didn't have Uncle Pete go to the party, would you be dead?" Evan asked round eyed.

"It's a good possibility. Dr. Jackson said Uncle Pete saved my life and I believe it." Smiling she tousled his hair. "But you know what? It was God that kept me from dying because he wants your mom and I to help keep other people safe. She saved a lot of people from getting hurt like I did when she became the inventor of Caution Clings."

"Cool, my mom's a 'ventor!" Evan called to his grandparent's.

"That's 'inventor', and I think it's pretty cool too." Cassie grinned as Evan pulled her arm.

"Are you still the lifeguard?"

"Yes, but sometimes I'm going to swim too," she laughed.

"Mom says I can swim. Are ya gonna swim with me?" Evan pleaded.

"In a bit, I need to talk with these guys for a while, then I'll come in for a few minutes. Okay?" Cassie pulled the robe back over her shoulders.

"Okay, Is Logan gonna swim?" He automatically looked around for him and Cassie grinned. In the short time Evan had known Logan they had become fast friends.

"No, Logan's not here today, but next time he comes he might swim."

"Good, I like 'im. Mom said I might get ta call 'im Uncle L-"

"Okay that's enough Evan," Jenna hastily hushed her son with a finger on his lips. "If you're going to swim you'd better get changed." After shooing him into the house she turned apologetically to her sister who was looking at her with a mock outraged expression.

"Really Jenna. Discussing my relationship with a child."

"Sorry Cass," Jenna blushed. "I'm afraid he must have overheard Bob and I talking. If Logan has a hard time popping the question he could have Evan do it. That boy has no sense of privacy."

"Apparently no one else in this family does either." Cassie tried to scowl as she eyed her family, but she couldn't quite pull it off. "How did you know I was swimming?"

Jenna blushed as she glanced at her mother who was looking decidedly guilty.

"I thought so," Cassie grinned. "Well, I'm glad Mom called you. Sit down, there's something I wanted to discuss with all of you."

Taking a deep breath she plunged in. "I'm thinking about not finishing the treatment schedule Dr. Jackson's laid out for me."

In the moment of shocked silence that followed her announcement a songbird trilled. Its sweet melody broke the stillness and every one rushed to speak at once. Cassie held her hands up and gave them all a radiant smile.

"I know, I know, I've been living for this for so long, but now I can see that it may not be what God has for me. I've waited for a miracle cure for ten years and now that it is on the horizon I'm wondering whether it's really all that important any more."

Carefully she explained her conversation with Serena to her family.

Rev. Hanson listened to her while Evan played nearby in the pool. It had been years since he had seen his daughter this animated. And when she told them of the way she had led the salesgirl to Christ he began to see the young woman who had, in her youth, talked of becoming a missionary. He knew she would soon ask his advice and prayed that what he told her would be of use, not only to her, but also to God.

"So, you see, I'm wondering if I should remove the very witnessing tool that I've been given." Cassie looked at her father. "Part of me wants nothing more than to erase all the evidence of the last ten years and the other part wants to use it for God's glory. What do you think I should do?"

Jonathan Hanson, the father, looked deep into his daughter's questioning eyes and what he saw there caused Rev. Hanson, the pastor, to answer. "I can't tell you what to do in this circumstance Cassie. I can only help you to see the options as clearly as possible. On one hand you are a beautiful young woman with the possibility of having a family in the not too distant future. And, as such I'm sure you would prefer to have the unsightly scars removed." He smiled at Cassie's blush.

"On the other hand you feel a calling in your life in which you feel the scars would be an effective witnessing tool. And somewhere in the middle is the heretofore unspoken desire to test a piece of equipment, which may in the future help many others who have also been scarred. Is that right?"

Cassie nodded. "Yes. You make the options seem very clear." She looked around with troubled eyes. "But what should I do? Remove them or leave them there?"

"I think you're missing something." Bob surprised everyone by speaking up. "I believe there's one option that has been overlooked."

"What could that be?" Jenna asked clearly puzzled.

"I don't think you will be showing all of your scars when you witness to someone, unless you are going to wear your swimsuit around everywhere," he grinned. "You could have the treatments on the scars that don't usually show and leave your arm for witnessing."

Melissa smiled at her son-in-law. "What a wonderful suggestion Bob, it's the best of both worlds so to speak."

"I think you're all forgetting something else," Jenna spoke up. "As Dad pointed out you may soon be in a position in which there will be another person involved with your future. I don't think you should do anything without consulting Logan first."

Cassie blushed again, "You're right. I was just asking for your advice. I wasn't planning on making any decision yet."

"Well, we gave you some options to think about, but the best advice anyone can give is to pray about it." Cassie's father squeezed her hand. "And we'll be praying too little one."

Evan had been watching the proceedings at poolside and when he saw the group begin to move about he called excitedly. "Aunt Cassie, are you gonna swim now?"

"You bet." Smiling, she dropped her robe and headed for the diving board.

Bob called Evan over and explained to the boy about Cassie's treatments. "Aunt Cassie's skin is still pretty sore so I don't want you pulling or hanging on her, understand?"

"Sure Dad, I'll be careful." Evan smiled happily as he went to join his aunt. They had fun and he only had to be reminded twice to be careful.

Later that afternoon when Logan called, Cassie avoided telling him about her swimming and her ideas concerning the treatments. Instead she visited with him concerning her family and the work he was doing in France.

"I wish you were here." Logan sighed. "The secretary they gave me is efficient enough, but she's not able to keep up with me like you do."

"Are you giving her a hard time?"

"I'm not trying to, but I guess you have me spoiled. You always know where everything is and what I need without my telling you."

"Oh dear, that poor woman must be ready to pull her hair out." Her amusement was evident. "You can be a bit difficult to work for, you know?"

"I'm a paragon among bosses," he teased. "I'm patient, kind and unassuming."

Laughing she picked up where he left off. "Not to mention hot headed, impatient and as grouchy as a bear with a sore head."

"Am I that bad?"

"Only on your good days."

"It's a wonder you've put up with me for so long," he said dryly.

"Everyone has his own cross to bear," she laughed. "The fringe benefits do out weigh the trials. Anyone who works with you also benefits from your incredible business sense. Not to mention your magnetic personality."

"Don't forget my boyish good looks."

"I haven't, believe me I haven't." Her voice was so full of longing that Logan nearly upset his well-laid plans and asked her to marry him right then and there. Changing the subject seemed to be the most prudent thing to do at this point, so he grabbed at the first thing that came to mind.

"Do you think you could help me with a small problem I'm having over here?"

"Sure what is it?"

He launched into the description of a situation he had dealt with earlier in the day and they soon had it sorted out.

"That's what's wrong, I only have half my brain with me. And here I thought I only had a hard time keeping my thoughts straight when you are close."

"You speak the most wonderful nonsense." Cassie laughed.

"It isn't nonsense," he argued. "Would you mind my calling you if I'm having difficulty straightening things out?"

"Sure, anytime!"

"Great." He grinned and drawled, "I was thinking..."

"Oh no, here we go again. Yes?"

"Well..."

"Hmm, Would that be an oil well or a water well?" she chuckled. "You do know that a well can be a very deep subject?"

"You're interrupting again."

"Am I?"

"Yes. Now, I was thinking."

"How difficult for you."

"You have no idea."

"Oh, I have an inkling," she laughed.

"Maybe it wouldn't be such a good idea after all," he said with a mock sigh. "I'm afraid you're far too distracting."

"For what?"

"For anything that involves being near you or within the sound of your voice." She could clearly hear the strain he was under.

"I'm sorry Logan," she was instantly contrite. "I won't tease you anymore."

"No, that's not the problem." His low voice was warm. "I like your sense of humor. It's one of my favorite things about you."

Relief flooded over Cassie leaving her light headed. "Just one? So, what are the other things?"

"Mmm, if I told you that you would have a decidedly big head." Her laughter coursed through him deliciously like the effervescence in sparkling water.

"Am I supposed to believe that nonsense?"

"Of course, I wouldn't attempt to fool you about the important things in life."

"Like, my big head? Logan you aren't making any sense."

"I'm afraid I've made precious little sense since for quite some time now." Shaking his head he continued. "Anyway to get back to the main subject. I was thinking that if you kept the cell phone with you I could call you about some of the more sticky situations that may arise here."

"I thought you were joking about that. Won't your secretary get offended?"

"Are you kidding?" He laughed. "I think she would probably kiss your feet if you got me off her back."

"Ah yes, I remember those days." She joined his laughter. "I do admit though that they didn't last that long. You acclimatized pretty quickly."

"Yes well, I had a lot of help from a pretty redhead."

"My hair's not red," she argued. "It's auburn."

"One with freckles that she kept hidden." He pushed the issue. "Although I don't remember seeing much of the fabled redheaded temper."

"I learned a long time ago to pick my battles," she grinned amused. She had prayed for a good job for too many years to waste it all on one stubborn boss who couldn't find what was laying right in front of his nose. Even if he was devastatingly good looking he had gotten on her nerves sometimes. Then one day she'd seen tried humor in her dealings with him and everything slid into perspective. After that it wasn't so hard to keep on an even keel with him.

"Somehow the idea of you picking battles sounds ominous," he mused.

"About as ominous as a poodle barking at a St. Bernard." From the strangled laughter coming over the phone lines she guessed he was as amused at her nonsense as she was at his.

"So which one am I?" He asked when he finally got his breath.

"If you don't already know, *I'm* not going to tell you," she said primly.

"Okay Fifi."

"Fifi! What an awful name!" She choked. "Logan don't you dare call me that in front of people."

"Hey you made the analogy, I didn't." Laughing he continued to tease her until she caught sight of the time.

"Oh my goodness, do you have any idea what time it is?"

"Of course, it's late enough you should probably be helping your mother with supper."

"You are the most wonderfully exasperating man I've ever met. And you need to get some sleep you must be exhausted."

"Talking with you can be very restful, of course, it can also be quite enlightening." There was true regret in his voice as he agreed with her that it was time to get some sleep. Logan never tired of listening to her, but he didn't want to run the risk that she would get tired of him. Praying together was the natural conclusion to their conversation.

Logan chuckled as he hung up the phone.

"Good night Fifi."

Chapter 11

"I can't believe I'm getting married in only eight days." Serena shook her head as she smoothed her hands over the satin incasing her slender waist. The sculptured neckline was decorated with a myriad of seed pearls that adorned the lace overlay of the bodice and the lacy cutaways along the hemline and short train. The sleeves were overlaid with the same lace and pearls and stopped just above the elbow leaving her forearms and dainty hands exposed.

"Reality will set in about the time you cut the cake," Jenna smiled. "So don't be surprised if everything seems slightly surreal."

"You are going to be the most beautiful bride to ever walk down the isle. I love how this dress flows when you move." Cassie's eyes shone as she watched her friend slowly twirl in front of the mirror.

"It's perfect Jenna, absolutely perfect." Serena's eyes grew misty as she took Jenna's hands. "It's exactly what I wanted."

"Thank you. It will take very little alteration. I could have it ready this afternoon if you'd like."

"How wonderful." Serena smiled. "There is only one more thing I'd like to see."

"What is that?"

"I want to see Cassie in her dress." She ignored Cassie's red face and sputtered protest. "You must have one picked out. With a sister who designs such beautiful creations I know you must have a dream dress."

"She does. Come on Cass," Jenna pleaded. "Just try it on."

"Oh all right," she sighed. "I'll try it on, but don't get any bright ideas. I've about had it with the crazy advice you two keep giving me."

"It's not *all* crazy, and you don't listen to us anyway." Jenna sighed and exchanged a conspiratorial smile with Serena as Cassie disappeared into the dressing room of Jenna's dress shop.

Jenna went to help her sister dress as Serena experimented in the mirror with her hair and the veil she had picked out.

When Cassie finally made an appearance, Serena gasped. "Oh my dear girl, you are lovely." Tears sprang to her eyes, as Cassie stood before her in a delicate dress that was perfect for her.

A high sweetheart neckline swept up to a short stand up collar at the back of her neck. Pearl encrusted lace covered the bodice and trailed down the waistline. The full skirt was sprinkled with sequins and tiny crystals, which sparkled when she moved. Long fitted sleeves encased her arms and spilled over her wrists.

"Aunt Cassie, you look like a princess!" Evan spoke the words they were all thinking.

Cassie hugged the little boy and Jenna saw a picture perfect photo opportunity. Snatching up her digital camera, which she kept nearby, she started taking snap shots of them modeling and acting silly. They discussed hair and accessories and the different merits of the veils Jenna had on display. Then Serena picked up the camera and took some beautiful shots of Cassie and Jenna.

"You should get some good advertisement photos out of these shots." Serena enthused.

"Just do me a favor and hide the ones with me in them. I wouldn't want Logan to run across them and think I'm hinting about marriage." Cassie worried.

"Mum's the word. I'll print them myself so you won't have to worry about any one getting wind of what we are doing." Jenna grinned delightedly. "It's too bad the timing is off because you two should have a double wedding."

"Oh Cassie wouldn't that be perfect?" Serena's eyes shone.

"It would be wonderful, but it's not going to happen," Cassie sighed wistfully and smiled. "Besides, you need to shine alone on that day, Serena. I wouldn't want anything to detract from your happiness."

"It would make me very happy to share my joy with my new son and his wife," Serena assured her. "When is Logan coming home?"

"In two days, he should be flying in late Sunday night and will be back at work on Monday morning." Cassie's cheeks grew warm at the thought of Logan's return.

"Well I for one will be happy when he gets back so you'll quit wandering around like a lost puppy and checking that cell phone every ten minutes," Jenna teased.

"The phone! Oh dear I forgot it in the dressing room." Cassie dashed off to the dressing room.

"Watch out for that dress!" Jenna called after her. Turning to Serena she gave her a watery smile. "I haven't seen her this happy in so long. Are you sure Logan's planning something?"

"Yes," Serena smiled. "I'm just not exactly sure what yet, but from what Theo tells me, those two had better get it together soon or they're going to fall apart at the seam's."

"What's going on in Paris?"

Serena laughed. "Theo says there wasn't really a need for Logan to go in the first place, but he stirred things up so badly by going over there that it's taking forever to get everything straightened out."

"Ah, we figured something fishy was happening."

"Jenna, can you help me out of this thing?" Cassie called from the back of the house.

"I'm coming, just let me check the fit of the dress," she said as she came into the dressing room.

"Why? I don't need a fitting." Cassie said suspiciously.

"Bob is taking me to the charity ball next month and I wanted to make a dress like this in a different fabric, of course. Since we are the same size I wanted to make sure it will fit right." Jenna was thinking fast and trying to come up with a plausible answer. "You know how hard it is for me to get the right fit on myself."

As Jenna talked she was making marks on the dress with chalk and sending up a prayer at the same time. The story she had told wasn't exactly a lie. She just hadn't told Cassie that her dress was already made.

As Jenna was helping Cassie out of her dress she suddenly sat down on the small bench and put her head between her knees.

"What's wrong?" Cassie reached for her sister.

"I'm just a little lightheaded, I forgot to eat breakfast." Jenna was quite flushed.

"Do you have a fever?" Cassie placed her hand on her sister's forehead. "No. What?" She asked quizzically.

"Oh!" She gasped. "Are you?"

"Well…" Jenna colored.

"Congratulations!" Cassie hugged her.

"Don't tell anyone! Mom and Dad don't even know yet."

"I promise I won't say anything." Cassie crossed her heart. "Can I get you something to eat?"

Jenna insisted she would be fine and that she kept a supply of snacks in the small kitchen.

By the time Cassie and Serena had changed back into street clothes. They were ready for lunch and they encouraged Jenna to come with them. She declined, and sent them off so she could have some peace and quiet.

Against their better judgement, Cassie and Serena left her and went to a nearby restaurant where they were soon immersed in wedding plans. Cassie had helped Jenna with several of their friend's weddings so she was able to offer some valuable advice.

Serena took notes and asked Cassie her opinion on many subjects. When pressed Cassie admitted that she thought the gazebo in the town square was the perfect setting for a wedding and Serena, who agreed, decided to check out the possibility.

Cassie's eyes shone as she explained how they could decorate the gazebo. She mentioned that the lovely gardens would be a perfect background for pictures. She even had practical ideas on where the serving tables could be set up and how the chairs should be arranged.

Serena took many of her suggestions and drew diagrams, asked questions about catering and music, and made notes until she was satisfied that she had all the information she could get. Then they headed to City Hall to check on permits. Between the two of them they covered a lot of ground and soon they were back at Jenna's picking up the dress and saying goodbye.

"Now don't forget to be at the park next Saturday by two o'clock for pictures. There's still so much to be done and I'll need your help." Serena reminded them as she got in her car. "Jenna I don't know how I can ever thank you for everything you're doing. I'll gladly tell everyone about you."

"Thank *you* Serena. I'll see you a week from tomorrow. Don't worry everything will turn out perfect, Good-bye." Jenna called as she and Cassie waved to the departing car.

"I like your future mother-in-law." Jenna smiled as they walked back to the house.

"You're going to feel mighty foolish if Logan and I don't get married." Cassie once again told her sister.

"I told you-"

"I know, you have a feeling and more than anything I hope you're right." Cassie said absently as she stared at the cell phone in her hand for the hundredth time in the last hour."

"You could call him you know." Jenna suggested.

"I know, but I don't want to disturb him. He said he would be in a meeting all day today. I just want to be available if he needs me."

"Honey, you are the most available woman I've ever met," Jenna grinned. "Have you ever tried playing hard to get?"

"Oh Jen, I couldn't do that."

"What happened to the cool sophisticated woman I saw at the office the day Evan and I stopped by?"

"She's gone. I can't pretend with Logan anymore. He knows how I feel and if he wants to take our relationship farther, it's up to him. I've left it all in God's hands and if this is what He has for me, then He will work it out or give me another job."

"That's an admirable attitude," Jenna was thoughtful. "What will you do if he doesn't ask you to marry him?"

"I'll be fine."

"Cassandra Joy Hanson, tell the truth."

Cassie made a valiant effort to act self assured, but failed miserably. "Well, Jennifer Elizabeth Thompson, if that's the case, I'm afraid I may shrivel up and die for awhile. Then I'll pull myself up by the bootstraps and go on."

"Now that's my sister talking." Jenna smiled.

Chapter12

Logan settled down in the taxi for the ride to his apartment. The long flight from Paris had been uneventful, but when he'd finally reached Boston he'd had a difficult time keeping his impatience at bay. Security had been tight at both ends of his flight causing many delays and he was eager to continue on with his plans. He was very tempted to tell the driver to take him directly to Jasonville, but he forced himself to keep to the course he had decided upon.

Dumping his luggage inside the door of his apartment he collapsed into a chair and said a quick prayer. Asking the Lord to give him strength and guidance he pulled out his cell phone and called Cassie.

"Logan?"

"Cassie, it's so good to hear your voice."

"Rough day?"

Logan smiled, "You have no idea."

"Is there anything I can help you with."

"How quickly can you get here?"

"Not all that quickly," she chuckled. "Tell me about your day."

"I don't want to think about my day," he hedged. "Tell me about yours."

Logan slowly relaxed as Cassie regaled him with the more humorous parts of her day with Serena. She carefully left out all mention of her own involvement with the wedding dresses. He laughed as she described the way Serena had reacted to Evan. Borrowing his baseball cap, she had fashioned a veil out of it and she and Evan had posed for pictures with his bat and ball.

The more he listened to this incredible woman the more he wanted to spend the rest of his life with her. He wondered if she was ready to take their relationship to the next level…marriage. He had prayed diligently about the emotional pain she had endured. And he knew that when he asked her to marry him, if there was any fear or reticence of any kind in her eyes, then they must, against his wishes, have a long engagement. The last thing he wanted was to push her into something she wasn't ready for.

Smiling he remembered the words of Louie, the head of the Paris branch of Blake International, after yesterday's meeting. Yesterday? It seemed a lot longer than that.

"Thankyou for your help Mr. Blake. I hope your time spent here was worth being away from your delightful assistant." Louie had smiled. "I cannot help but wonder why you would not bring the woman you love to the most romantic city in the world."

Logan hadn't been too surprised to find that the intuitive man knew of his love for Cassie, but it had taken some time to explain the situation to him. Louie, with the heart of a true romantic, understood the situation precisely and had insisted on Logan flying out early so he could surprise her. He maintained that if Logan looked into her eyes the moment she saw him the answer he was looking for would be clearly visible for him to see.

Logan certainly hoped that was true. Well, he would find out tomorrow. But first he must get through tonight.

"Logan?" Cassie's voice broke in on his concentration. "Are you sleeping?"

"No, but I'm dreaming." Logan smiled.

"Of what?"

"Not what, who." Logan chuckled as he deliberately teased her.

Cassie blushed scarlet as she choked back a laugh. "Hey, keep your mind on the subject."

"I am," he muttered much to her delight.

Her trill of laughter danced along his spine sparking an emotion so great that he clung to the telephone like a lifeline. Breathing deeply he forced himself to relax and laugh with her.

"So what else has Evan been up to, besides being in an impromptu photo shoot?"

"He's having a great time swimming and trying to out race Susan with the remote controlled cars." Cassie grinned as she remembered how quickly Sadie's daughter had learned how to control the toys.

"Trying? I'll have to have a talk with him about not trying too hard. Sometimes it's more prudent to allow the girl to win."

"Oh?" Cassie drawled. "Are you saying that when we raced, you let me win?"

"Of course not, but there is more than one way to win." Logan couldn't help testing the waters a little.

"I'm just saying that there are times when a man needs to follow the woman's lead." He was deliberately baiting her hoping she would let something slip and he would be able to tell how far she had come in her emotional healing. "As you know, there is a lot to be learned from watching a person's response."

Who was he watching? Had he met someone else? A cold hand clutched at her heart as she tried to make sense of the stab of pain that ripped through her leaving her vulnerable. Speaking slowly she tried to keep all trace of jealousy out of her voice as she tried a little fishing of her own.

"There's also a lot to be learned by listening. Sometimes when we are talking your thoughts are a thousand miles away."

"There are times," his voice was low. "When a man's thoughts should only be spoken of in person. And even then words aren't always necessary."

Relief flooded through her causing her to feel lightheaded as she felt the familiar warmth flooding her system. She wasn't quite sure what was happening, but she once again longed to feel the security of his arms around her.

"How far away are you?" She was as surprised by her question as he was.

"Too far," his deep chuckle rolled over her.

"Mmm, Do you have to wait until Sunday to fly in?" There was a definitely flirtatious quality to her voice that she hadn't heard for so long that she wondered where it came from. She realized that she was playing with fire, but she needed assurance that he still felt the same desire for her that he did the night of her birthday. She continued cautiously wading into uncharted waters. "I-I hope I'll see you before Monday morning."

"If I don't see you before then, we could always lock the door of the office and put up a 'Do not disturb' sign." He closed his eyes as he fought to subdue the thoughts that came unbidden to his mind.

"That could be dangerous," she laughed deliciously, secure in the knowledge that he was indeed going through the same torment that she was. "We might never want to open it again."

"Never?" Even though she had assured him before that she wasn't afraid of him Logan still felt an overwhelming desire to make certain. "Are you sure you wouldn't be afraid to be alone with me?"

A beautiful smile lit her face as she spoke the simple words that brought joy to his hungry heart. "I could never be afraid of you."

For a moment Logan couldn't breathe, so great was the relief that flooded over him. He was filled with thanksgiving as he whispered a heartfelt and very shaky, "Thank you!"

Chapter 13

Logan tried to keep his impatience in check as he cautiously maneuvered his way through the morning traffic. He had given himself plenty of time knowing that this would be one of the most important meetings of his life and it wouldn't do to lose patience now.

At precisely ten o'clock he was greeted by a smiling Rev. Hanson and led into the small office where he had so explosively interrupted Dr. Jackson's proposal for Cassie's treatment.

"Thank you for seeing me Rev. Hanson. I appreciate you keeping quiet about our meeting."

"In this instance I agree that it was best kept quiet. What can I do for you?"

Logan took a deep breath and looked squarely at Rev. Hanson. "I'd like your honest opinion on how Cassie is doing."

"For the most part, she's doing very well. The treatment she received was, I thought, a bit too extensive, but she had her reasons for trying to get it over with as soon as possible."

"Yes, my father agrees that she had too large an area done at once, but when I talk to her she won't admit to being in pain, she just keeps saying that she's fine." The worry that crept into Logan's voice warmed Rev. Hanson's heart and he decided to speak frankly.

"Physically Cassie's in better shape than I've seen her in years." Rev. Hanson smiled as he watched the play of emotions on the face of the man before him. "Spiritually I've seen marked growth. This last week she's been spending time with the Church youth group and has helped the kids with their fundraiser to offset the cost of going to camp next month," he smiled fondly. "Every chance she gets she admonishes the young ones to think like Christians. I'm very proud of her, but there's still something missing."

Logan's brows contracted. "Missing? She sounds like she's getting along fine." *Without me,* the thought came unbidden to his mind, causing the crushing weight of loneliness to weigh upon him.

Rev. Hanson prayed for guidance as he leaned forward and looked at Logan man to man.

"I've watched Cassie this past week, she's like a cat on a hot tin roof. Her smile is there, but sometimes it seems to slip. Often she stares into space as if she's miles away." His concern was obvious. "Her mother and I thought we had lived through the worst possible pain. Watching our daughter escape death only to be dreadfully scarred was torture. Then we found out there were worse things than surface scarring. We saw her go from a bright outgoing young woman, to a withdrawn frightened individual who was determined not to let the world see her as vulnerable."

"About three months after the accident she suddenly closed in on herself." Shaking his head he continued. "It was as if she was simply afraid to live. She wouldn't talk to us. She quit every school and church activity and immersed herself in her studies. At graduation she was asked to give a speech and she just shuddered and refused. We were so worried about allowing her to go away for college, but she insisted she wanted to go somewhere no one knew her, so we agreed."

"I watched my daughter become what could only be described as a 'plastic' person. When I tried to talk to her she answered all my questions as if she knew the answers by heart, but there was no joy left to animate her features." He smiled sadly as he watched the reaction his words had on Logan.

"Then a couple of years after she started working for your company, I began to see a subtle difference in her. I would still find her staring into space so engrossed with her own thoughts that she didn't notice anything or anyone, but this time there was a softness around her eyes and mouth. I wondered if she was dating someone, but she denied it. Then the day she got the job as your assistant, things really began to change. Over the last two years we saw her slowly emerge from the depths of a depression that had seemed endless." Chuckling over the memories of those days he continued. "She quoted you so often that we began to feel as if we knew you."

"That day when Jenna came home with a crazy story about you two falling off the desk, I knew that what I had been praying for had finally happened. When you walked in on Dr. Jackson's proposal my hopes were more than confirmed."

Smiling across the desk Rev. Hanson continued. "I want you to know that you have played a big part in bringing my Cassie back to life and I'll always be grateful to God that he brought a man of integrity into our lives." Leaning back in his chair he smiled encouragingly. "I'm sure you didn't come here to listen to me ramble. Thanks for hearing me out, but I believe you have something you wanted to say."

"Well sir, thank you for you're confidence, but I believe the lion's share of credit for Cassie's recovery goes to your family. You've been there for her each step of the way with your prayers and encouragement."

"Cassie's work ethics have been exemplary. I couldn't have found a better assistant and I wish all my workers were a fraction as diligent." Logan smiled. "The first time I saw her across the room two and a half years ago, I was..." He chuckled at the memory. "Thunderstruck. I checked with her supervisor and found her to be as smart as she is beautiful. So when she applied for the job as my assistant there was really no contest," he smiled sheepishly. "She was the only one who got an interview."

"Eventually when Cassie started letting her guard down, we became friends, but I couldn't get past the walls she had erected to keep anyone from getting too close. I was praying for a miracle when Evan's spider came to call. The Lord knew exactly what was needed to send me up on that desk with her."

Logan looked earnestly at the big man across from him. "I fell in love with Cassie the first time I saw her. It has just about been the death of me waiting for her to heal enough inside and out so she could put the past behind her and start looking toward the future. I'm not sure how long it will take before she's ready to let go and move on." He took a long steadying breath and said, "but I know I can't live much longer without her so sir, I'm asking for your daughter's hand in marriage."

The ticking of the old-fashioned mantle clock on top of the bookcase was as loud as a drumbeat in the quiet of the room. A splash from the pool outside broke the stillness. Rev. Hanson got up and walked to the window where he stood looking through the blinds into the backyard.

Logan prayed silently, He had bared his soul to this man in hopes that he would see how much he loved Cassie and when the time was right he would give them permission to marry.

When Rev. Hanson finally turned toward Logan he had tears in his eyes and his face worked convulsively as he smiled.

"There is no one on this earth I'd rather have marry my daughter."

Logan rose to shake the hand that the Reverend held out to him.

"You have been worried that she hasn't healed yet." Cassie's father motioned to the window. "Well, you tell me what you think."

The scene before him stunned Logan. Cassie was standing on the diving board with her face turned to the sun and her arms outstretched. As he watched she walked to the end, turned and executed a perfect back dive. Emerging with a smile she swam to the edge and pulled herself gracefully from the pool. Drying her hands on a fluffy beach towel, she checked the ever-present cell phone for messages before returning to the water.

"That phone has been her life line," Cassie's father continued. "This past week everything has revolved around your calls. Come with me."

Leading the way to the spare bedroom he motioned to a large dresser. "There are spare swimsuits in the bottom drawer. I'm sure Cassie would love having your company." Glancing at his watch he smiled. "I don't want to be rude, but Melissa and I have a lunch date and won't be back for a couple of hours. If you get hungry there's food in the refrigerator."

"Thank you for your trust." Logan shook Rev. Hanson's hand and looked solemnly into the older man's eyes. A bond forged between them in that instant.

As Cassie's parents left the house. There was no remaining doubt that Logan was the right one for their daughter

* * *

Cassie had just checked the phone for the third time since coming outside and Logan still hadn't called. What was going on? It was after four o'clock in Paris and last Saturday Logan had called her before now. Surely it hadn't taken this long to wrap things up. She moved restlessly in the lounge chair, she'd never get a tan if she kept flopping around like a fish out of water.

Hmm, a fish out of water was an apt simile for how she'd been feeling these past two weeks while Logan was gone. The first week working with Theo had been difficult enough, but this past week had been increasingly torturous. Just knowing that Logan might call at any minute had her nerves in a constant state of panic. Once again she prayed for his safe return. If only he would call so she knew everything was on schedule, then maybe she could begin to relax.

Ah, exactly who was she kidding? She knew she wouldn't relax until she was once again in Logan's arms. Her love for him was growing every day and she was trying to be patient. The Bible said something about trials bringing patience. Well, it's a wonder she doesn't have all the patience in the world with the trials she'd gone through. She made a mental note to look up that scripture, just to make sure she wasn't missing something important.

When the telephone finally rang Cassie nearly jumped out of her skin. Scrambling for the phone she took a deep breath before answering it.

"Cassie?" Logan's rich tones flowed over her like a balm. "Are you okay? You sound out of breath."

"I'm fine. Did you get everything finished up over there?"

"Pretty much. Louie can finish the rest with no problems. Do you miss me?"

"Yes," her simple answer warmed his heart.

"When can I see you."

Cassie's tinkling laugh held a slight edge as she used his words. "How quickly can you get here?"

"You'd be surprised. I can be mighty speedy when I want to be," he teased.

"Do you? Want to be, I mean."

"Very much so. When can I pick you up?" He grinned, thinking of the last time that he had played this game with her.

"I could meet you at the airport." She stood when she heard the opening of the sliding glass door, but not looking forward to the interruption, she didn't turn.

"I think it would be quicker if I met you at your parent's house. Say, by the pool?"

Cassie's heart began to beat a rapid tattoo. Her inner radar was going crazy. Somehow the impossible had happened and he was there. Afraid she was mistaken she closed her eyes and whispered, "when?"

"How about now?" his voice reached her ears without benefit of the cell phone and slowly she lowered the phone. He took it from her nerveless fingers and placed it on the table. Then he gently lifted her chin and whispered huskily, "Open your eyes."

Tears pricked her eyes as she slowly opened them. The piercing blue of his gaze probed her emerald depths, confirming the words that she had spoken last night. There was no trace of fear to be seen, only love, as he pulled her into his arms and held her as if he would never let her go.

Caught off guard, there was no room for pretense or politeness. Cassie clung to him as tears left their trail down her cheeks. One arm was wrapped around his neck and with the other hand she ruffled his hair and felt the slight roughness of his cheek as she made sure he was really there.

He gently rained kisses over her face tasting the salt from her tears. When their lips finally met the earth stood still.

Eventually, Cassie realized that Logan was dressed in swimming trunks and a T-shirt.

"You *are* here," she breathed as she clutched his shoulders.

"Mmm, finally," his arms tightened and he rubbed his cheek against her hair.

"Why didn't you tell me you were coming early?"

"I wanted to surprise you," he grinned down at her. "And Louie threw me out of France before I made an even bigger mess of his company." Logan chuckled as he remembered Louie's face as he laughingly told his boss not to come back without Cassie.

"I'll have to thank him," she smiled back, then she gasped turning crimson as she tried to step away. "My parents! They're probably watching us."

Shaking his head, Logan refused to let her go. "Your father told me they had a lunch date and they left before I called you," he smiled. "I have a feeling they were being tactful." He brushed his hands gently over her back and shoulders. "Are you okay? Did I hurt your back?"

"Not a chance," Cassie smiled. "Dr. Jackson is surprised at how quickly I've healed." Cassie pulled her braided hair over her shoulder and turned in his arms baring her back to him. "What do you think?"

"You know what I think Beautiful," he whispered as he kissed her shoulder.

Cassie shuddered under his touch, as she struggled not to lean back against him. She had known that the feel of his lips could make her go weak at the knees, but this was something deliciously different and she knew she would have to move soon.

"Cassie?"

"Yes?" She murmured.

"I…" With a sigh Logan forced himself to release her. He knew that he must put a little distance between them or there would be no stopping himself. "I thought you were swimming."

"I was." Turning to look at him, she tried to control her shaking hands as she tucked a stray curl behind her ear. This was madness, she wanted to be near him, but she knew better than to continue in the direction they were headed. Smiling brightly she threw out a challenge as she stepped to the edge of the pool. "Want to race?"

"You're on." Joining her, he loved her all the more for acting on his lead to put a lid on their rapidly escalating emotions. They determinedly kept the atmosphere light between them as they swam.

Later Cassie sent Logan to use the guestroom with its connecting bath as she quickly used her parent's shower.

Logan was in the kitchen pouring glasses of iced tea when Cassie walked in wearing the dress she bought the day she had lunch with Serena. He drew a sharp breath and let it out slowly.

"I'm glad you don't dress like this at the office. " He gave her a swift kiss as if he were afraid to let his lips linger. "You make a fine distraction."

Cassie smiled at Logan's silliness as she started pulling things from the refrigerator. With his help she quickly put together a feast of succulent chicken sandwiches, crisp green salad and fresh fruit. They kept up a lighthearted conversation while they ate, but during clean up their talk turned to serious matters when Logan asked about Cassie's treatment.

"I believe, when it's fully tested, the M-1 will prove to be quite effective."

"Now that sounds like one of the reports sent in by research and development." Logan looked closely at her. "I'm waiting for the, *but*..."

"But, I'm trying to decide if I even want to continue the treatments."

"Was it too painful?"

"That's not the reason." She told him of her conversation with Serena and the way she had started using her scars to witness not only to people she met on the street, but also to the youth group at church.

"Do you think that this may have something to do with the message you received during your near death experience?" Logan inquired with interest.

"I'm not exactly sure, but I believe it is something I definitely want to explore." Cassie told him of the other options she had discussed with her family. "What do you think?"

"The final decision is up to you," he said thoughtfully. "You told me once that the treatments weren't medically necessary. Do the scars cause you any discomfort?"

"Some of the places on my back and legs have rather thick scaring and they have started pulling," she admitted.

"You may want to have those areas taken care of. I know you have been waiting a long time for this and if it's what you want to do, I'll help you in any way I can."

"Now *I'm* waiting for the, *but...*" Cassie grinned.

"But, I love you for who you are, scars and all." Logan pulled her into his arms and kissed her tenderly as he ran his hands over her back and shoulders. He gently fingered the ridges beneath the delicate silk of her dress. Soon the only coherent thought left to her was how much she loved him and didn't want to live another day without him.

When he released her lips he held her tightly in his arms, feeling their hearts beating as one.

And they shall be one flesh. The scripture from Genesis came unbidden to his mind. *One flesh.* Marriage.

Releasing her, he took a step back and clasped her hands. Looking deeply into her eyes that could one minute be as deep and serene as an emerald pond and the next as turbulent as the raging waters of the sea. Logan spoke what had been on his mind for as long as he had known her.

"I can't live like this anymore. Somehow I have to make you understand how I feel. I love the way you challenge me to be more than I am. I love how you always know what I need even before I ask. Being away from you has been nothing short of torture, it's like a vital part of me is missing and when we're together again I'm...complete. I want to pull you to me and never let you go. I ask your opinion on everything just so I can hear your voice." He dropped to one knee on the kitchen floor, as his voice growing husky with emotion. "I want to go to sleep every night with you in my arms and kiss you awake each morning as the sun comes up to caress your lovely face. I want you to be my partner in life's journey and the mother of my children. Won't you please marry me?"

"Yes! Oh Logan, yes!" Cassie knees buckled and she fell sobbing into his arms.

There, in the middle of the kitchen floor he sat leaning against the cabinets as he cradled her and kissed away all the worry and uncertainty of the past weeks.

After awhile Logan grinned. "My father will be happy. He threatened to come out of retirement if I didn't make you the daughter he never had."

"I think Serena will keep him busy for a long time to come." Cassie chuckled. "And Evan will be ecstatic that he can finally call you Uncle Logan."

"Uncle Logan, I think I like that almost as much as I'm going to like Daddy." He kissed her again tenderly. "How soon can you be ready to marry me?"

Cassie grinned, "How about a week?"

"That long?" Logan grinned, then asked puzzled. "Isn't that when Dad and Serena are getting married?"

"Serena and your father want us to have a double wedding. The guest list should be similar and I already have a minister." Cassie grinned impishly. "I've known him all my life and I hear he's very good."

"Since you recommend him, I'm sure he'll be fine. Besides," he teased, "I'll already be in a tux. We might as well kill two birds with one stone."

"Hey!" He ducked as she playfully swatted him.

Rev. and Mrs. Hanson found them still sitting on the kitchen floor laughing over their nonsense. Cassie's father smiled and asked, "Is this a private party, or a family affair?"

"Definitely family," Cassie laughed as Logan helped her up from the floor.

"I'm glad you're here," Logan smiled. "I need some witnesses, you see, Cassie has consented to marry me." Reaching into his pocket he pulled out a small jewelers box, and taking the ring from its velvet bed, slid it onto Cassie's finger where he sealed it with a kiss. "I want to make sure that this isn't just a dream." He dropped a kiss on her smiling lips then shook her father's hand while her mother hugged her tightly.

The doorbell rang and Melissa wiped her eyes as she hurried to answer it.

"I was hoping that our little impromptu lunch date would give you enough time to propose properly." Rev. Hanson smiled.

Logan grinned, "I held out as long as I could, but your daughter was too much for me."

"The Hanson women have that effect on you." Bob interjected as his family walked in. There was another round of hugs and congratulations as they were brought up to date on the news.

"It's a good thing I finished your dress today." Jenna smiled as she and Cassie placed lemonade on trays to be carried out to the patio. "Serena will be thrilled. She was just telling me that she hoped Logan would hurry up and ask you so you can get married at the same time."

"Has everyone in Jasonville and Boston been discussing my love life," Cassie asked amused.

"Almost, it's supposed to be announced on national television Monday morning," Jenna joked. "Oh, Susan is available to be the flower girl and Evan can be the ring bearer. And I almost have my matron of honor dress finished." She laughed at the look on Cassie's face. "What do you think Mom and I have been doing this past month?"

"Is Serena in on this too?" Cassie couldn't help asking.

"Why do you think she kept asking you so many questions and insisted you should try on your dress? *We* knew you would need a final fitting." Jenna laughed merrily as she picked up her tray. "By the way, I fixed your sleeves and your dress is perfect."

Cassie shook her head and smiled as she followed her sister outside.

Chapter 14

Two large RV's parked along the street in the Town Square for the wedding party. One was a temporary base for the grooms and the other doubled as the bride's room. Jenna and her assistant were in their element, as the wedding coordinators, with Melissa Hanson gallantly dividing her efforts between the two brides.

Photographers had been working overtime trying and get as many pictures done before the ceremony as possible. And now, as the wedding was about to begin, the female portion of the wedding party was assembled in a circle in the confines of the RV. They held hands in a billowing mass of satin; tulle and lace as Rev. Hanson led them in prayer asking the Lords blessing on the proceedings.

At the proper time Bob escorted his mother-in-law across the lawn and down the white runner to her seat in front of the gazebo. She ran a quick look over the setting to make sure everything was in order. The chairs were filled with what looked like the entire town of Jasonville, with at least half of Boston included.

Logan and Theo waited with Rev. Peterson, the minister from the church they and Serena attended in Boston. Bob and Dr. Jackson joined them at the altar, which was set up in the wisteria-draped gazebo awaiting their duties as best men. The flowering vine added a natural setting needing little additional decoration, but the white tent set up nearby had been strung with thousands of tiny golden lights. Tulle wrapped garlands of wisteria and other flowers that grew in the square were draped around the poles and tables laden with a vast array of catered dishes.

Melissa breathed a sigh of relief as she turned to watch Susan diligently sprinkle rose petals as she walked in time to the music, followed by Gina, Serena's close friend, and matron of honor.

Standing with the rest of the congregation, she watched as Serena emerged from the screen set up outside the RV on the arm of an old family friend. She was dramatically beautiful in her lace covered, satin gown with her bouquet of rich tiger lilies. The front of her thick, dark hair swept up into the clip on her veil, while the back was left to flow in deep curls over her shoulders. She paced slowly up the isle to stand beside an impatiently waiting Theo.

There was a pause, and the music swelled again, as everyone turned to watch Jenna make her smiling way down the isle.

Melissa's heart caught in her throat when Cassie appeared on her father's arm. Her hair was a cloud of auburn ringlets caught in a gold tiara with a waltz length veil hanging down her back. The sweetheart neckline was the perfect frame for the necklace and earrings Logan had given her for her birthday. The satin bodice, its lace adorned with tiny pearls, accentuated her slender waist. Sequins scattered with crystals across the full tulle skirt caught the rays of the setting sun, setting off a myriad of sparkling light as she moved. Clothed in Light…

Melissa heard a gasp and caught a movement out of the corner of her eye. She turned in time to see Theo take hold of Logan's arm, preventing him from rushing down the isle to meet his bride. His look of joy and awe was reflected in Cassie's smile as she approached. Pausing a moment she kissed her mother and father as Rev. Peterson began the ceremony.

Cassie's father took his place next to Rev. Peterson and he had the joy of joining his daughter and Logan in Holy matrimony. When the end of the ceremony drew near his voice cracked as he invoked God's blessings over the happy couple.

Darkness had fallen and a myriad of lights created a fairy tale setting as Logan and Cassie danced. The music was soft and dreamy and Cassie basked in the warm embrace of her husband.

Passing her new in-laws she smiled up into Logan's face and observed. "I couldn't have dreamed of a more perfect wedding."

"And I couldn't have asked for a more beautiful bride." Logan kissed the end of her nose and glanced around.

"Are you looking for someone?"

"No," he grinned. "I was thinking…"

"Here we go again," Cassie laughed.

"You're interrupting."

"Oh dear, I suppose I shouldn't do that," she smiled in mock meekness. "You might lose your train of thought."

"Hmm, that could have disastrous results." His arms tightened and he nuzzled her ear causing her heart to jump and warm color flush her cheeks. His low chuckle assured her that he knew exactly what he was doing.

"Stick to the subject," she admonished breathlessly.

"I am," he grinned. "I was thinking that it surely must be time for us to leave."

"I think that could be arranged," she smiled as she stopped next to Serena and Theo. From Serena's rosy glow, Cassie assumed that they were also ready to leave. A look of joy passed between father and son, and there were many hugs and kisses as Cassie's parents joined in.

Cassie and Serena descended on Jenna with many thanks for her efforts in making their day perfect. Cassie reminded Jenna again to stay off her feet and not to forget to eat. The bouquets were thrown and one last kiss made a perfect photo opportunity as cameras flashed around the happy couples.

Logan and Cassie took the brunt of the birdseed as they ran through the crowd to their waiting limousine. With a quick shake

Logan ushered Cassie through the door and they waved out the back window before settling down for the trip into the city.

Making the most of their ride they relaxed as they compared notes on the day; chuckling over Evans disgust at having to let Susan tuck her hand into his arm as he escorted her down the isle. Then with typical five and seven-year-old enthusiasm they had danced wildly and eaten everything in sight.

Logan had quietly made plans for their honeymoon and had as yet to tell her where they were going. When they pulled up in front of the Blake International building Cassie gave him a puzzled look, but at his urging she got out in a billowing cloud of tulle. And the security guard let them in with a smile and ushered them into the elevator.

Determined not to let her curiosity get the better of her, Cassie watched quietly while Logan firmly closed and locked the office door behind them. She followed him into his office and stood waiting as he swung open the door of his private suite.

The scent of flowers wafted out as she gasped at the scene before her. What had once been an ordinary executive hideaway had been transformed into a honeymoon suite. Bouquets of flowers and plants overflowed giving the place the look of a garden paradise.

Cassie turned wide eyes to Logan, then she smiled, remembering his suggestion that they hide out in the office when he returned from Paris.

"I hope you don't mind, but our flight to New Zealand doesn't leave until Monday morning." His voice was husky as he lifted her in his arms and carried her over the threshold. "We have plenty of food and I had our bags delivered here earlier." Kissing her deeply he let her down slowly until her feet were firmly on the ground.

When he released her she ruffled his hair. "I think it's perfect," she smiled.

Logan grinned. "I was thinking…"

"Yes?" she chuckled.

"Don't distract me Mrs. Blake." He laughed as he hung a sign on the door.

"I wouldn't dream of it Mr. Blake." Laughing she slid her arms around his neck.

"Where was I?"

"You were thinking," she reached up to kiss him.

"I think too much," he murmured as he pushed the door closed setting the 'Do not disturb' sign in motion.

Epilogue

Logan entered the hospital room with two packages, one wrapped in pink, and the other in blue. He placed them on the bed and kissed Cassie tenderly.

"How are you feeling?" he asked as she handed him the tightly wrapped bundle wearing a minute blue stocking cap.

"Happy," Cassie smiled as she watched her husband cradle his son. "Mark and I are ready to leave when you are. You just missed Dr. Jackson. He and Nurse Martha wanted to know when Serena and I would be ready to continue our treatments. I told them to come by after we get home.

"Don't do anything until you are ready. There's no big hurry since Dad and I found him some different test subjects." Logan stepped over to his father who was holding a similarly wrapped bundle in pink. "And how is my little sister today?"

"Marie is ready to go home too. Just like her mommy is." Theo kissed Serena who was watching her husband and daughter with indulgent eyes.

"You weren't leaving without us were you?" Jenna asked as she entered carrying one month old Emma.

"I still can't get over you two having your babies on the same day." Melissa Hanson exclaimed.

"We're very punctual," Serena grinned. "But, it is odd that we both delivered on our nine month anniversary."

"I don't think anyone's going to believe this wasn't planned." Theo stated over the laughter.

"Oh it was planned alright." Rev. Hanson smiled. "Our heavenly Father knows exactly when babies are supposed to be born."

"I'm just glad they are all healthy." Jenna voiced the thoughts of each of them as the men handed the babies to their wives in wheelchairs.

It was quite a procession that wheeled into the lobby where a very excited little boy waited with his father. Evan's red head fairly danced with excitement.

"Uncle Logan, I got Mark a stuffed truck. Dad said I can't give 'im a real one cuz he's too little."

"Thank you Evan, I'm sure he'll love it." Logan smiled at his nephew.

"An' Gran'pa Theo, we got a doll for Marie." Evan used the honorary title as he handed Theo a package. "Susan said she can't have a truck till she get's grown up."

"Where is Susan?" Serena asked.

"She couldn't come to the hospital," Evan informed her importantly.

"Does she come over to visit Emma a lot?"

"Yeah, but she likes to drive the remote cars best," Evan announced. "She's coming over when we get home."

"Speaking of home, we'd better get these little ones on the road." Logan fussed as he pushed Cassie's wheelchair out to the waiting car and helped put his son into the well-tested safety seat.

Carefully he helped Cassie into the car then ran around to the opposite side and with a wave slid into the driver's seat. After checking on Mark, who was already asleep, he turned to Cassie.

"I was thinking…"

"You think too much," she grinned as their lips met in a kiss filled with the promise of many years to come.

www.ingramcontent.com/pod-product-compliance
Lightning Source LLC
Chambersburg PA
CBHW031533040426
42445CB00010B/517